AL DENTE

Maria Chiara Martinelli

AL DENTE

Photographs by Giorgio De Camillis

GREMESE
INTERNATIONAL

The Publisher would like to express very special thanks to the typically Italian restaurant *Otello alla Concordia* in Rome, for its staff's precious assistance in preparing the recipes photographed.
Also many thanks to the confectioner *Ghimenti* and to the restaurant *Al Ceppo* (photos pp. 27 and 54).

The photos on pages 12, 56, 82 and 172 were created by chef Antonio Sciullo who kindly contributed them for our use.

© 1996 Gremese International s.r.l.
P.O. Box 14335
00149 Rome

ISBN 88-7301-069-5

CONTENTS

INTRODUCTION

Famous the world over for its artistic treasures and natural beauty, Italy is of course equally renowned for its table. Indeed, if cooking is also an expression of the culture of a people, as we truly believe it is, then to consider only the historical and artistic heritage of a country without including its cuisine would be a great omission!

This is particularly true when it comes to Italy, whose cuisine is recognized as one of the best in the world. For in Italy, eating means much more than simply satisfying a biological necessity... it is also a voyage of discovery into the history, culture, and creativity of a people who, calling upon the resources of their imagination, have managed, sometimes with only a few simple ingredients, to create delicious specialties known and loved the world over.

Those who wish to become more thoroughly acquainted with the basics of Italian cuisine as well as discover its many secrets, will find their efforts greatly rewarded. The "insider's" perspective thus gained will help them to become truly selective and know precisely what, where, and how to appreciate the very best Italian cuisine has to offer whether traveling in Italy, eating out in Italian restaurants, or cooking at home.

The purpose of this volume is to give all lovers of Italian cuisine a complete panorama of its gastronomy: its distinctive features, its most typical products and dishes, as well as interesting cultural sidelights about the regions of Italy where they come from.

It offers a complete collection of the "most Italian" recipes that can easily be prepared at home by the foreign cook with precious hints on how to make these dishes truly genuine. And as you will note, most of the recipes in *Al Dente* include alternative ingredients for typical Italian products which might not always be readily available in all countries, though you will probably find most of the ingredients are widely distributed outside Italy.

What a wonderful way to discover this country and create the true atmosphere of a holiday in Italy right at home !

MAIN CHARACTERISTICS OF ITALIAN COOKING

Based principally upon ingredients typical of the Mediterranean region, Italian gastronomy originally developed out of a decidedly frugal diet. This was later influenced and embellished by the traditions of the wealthy courts that ruled Italy's regions over the centuries, as well as by convents and monasteries that often produced veritable culinary masterpieces, notably in pastry making. Gastronomically speaking, Italy can be divided into two quite distinct regions: the North, with its delicate flavors and greater use of butter; and the Center and South, where olive oil is preferred and dishes generally have a strong, often spicy-hot flavor. However, in recent years this distinction has gradually become less marked. Now increasingly common throughout the country are newly invented dishes which are not rooted in any specific regional tradition but are inspired – directly or indirectly – by the trends of *nouvelle cuisine.*

A great use of vegetables and aromatic herbs has always been common to the whole Peninsula, while spices are not heavily used except for pepper and, in the South, hot red chili peppers. Besides vegetables and herbs there is, of course, pasta, which, in its infinite variations has the amazing property of changing its taste according to its shape. If you were in Italy you would of course ask for your pasta to be served *al dente,* that is, at that perfect point when it is thoroughly cooked yet still firm – genuine Italian pasta! Nor would you have to settle for the most common sauces such as tomato or meat sauce, for there are infinite ways pasta can be prepared, an incredible variety of sauces and garnishings to be discovered. By carefully following the recipes in our collection, true Italian pasta will hold no secrets – providing, of course, it is never allowed to overcook!

Fish, shellfish, and seafood are also very much present in Italian cuisine, but they are often prepared very simply, usually grilled or poached, for example. There are, however, a few more elaborate preparations presented in our recipes. With regard to meat, all the regions of the Peninsula rely heavily on the use of pork, though there are also many traditional recipes for beef, particularly from central and southern Italy.

Italy also produces an impressive range of cheeses, cold cuts, bread, and wine. Every region, and even the different quarters of a city, produces typical specialities of its own, resulting in a great diversity of these foods.

Finally, there are many different kinds of desserts, sweets and pastries, often traditionally bound to certain religious holidays.

THE ITALIAN MENU

The typical Italian menu is comprised of four courses plus dessert.

Traditionally, the appetizer (*antipasto*) which begins the meal, is an assortment of cold cuts accompanied by olives and various pickled vegetables. However, there are many other warm and cold dishes also served as *antipasto*. The main idea of this course is that instead of one full portion, it is an assortment of various little tasters.

Then follows the first course, which is usually pasta or rice or a soup. At this point, the Italian culinary imagination really takes flight, more than at any other point in the meal, and the possibilities are delicious and exciting.

The second course is usually fish or meat and here again there is a considerable variety, with cooked greens or salad considered as separate side dishes. Before going directly on to dessert, there is usually a selection of assorted cheeses followed by fruit or fruit salad or ice cream (*gelato*) or some pastry.

It is always very pleasant to end the meal with an espresso coffee which is stronger and more aromatic than the coffee usually served in other countries.

This can be followed by an *amaro* (bittersweet liqueur), or other type of liqueur (see the section "Liqueurs").

Of course the elaborate menu described above is certainly not the typical everyday meal of Italians. Such meals are usually only prepared on holidays or when entertaining. Generally the rhythm of modern life has imposed much simpler and lighter meals consisting of a first course, generally *pasta asciutta* (dried pasta) served with a sauce rather than in a soup, a second course of meat or fish (or cold cuts or cheese) with a side dish of salad or a cooked vegetable, and, finally, fresh fruit.

When Italians or visitors decide to go out for a meal, Italy abounds in places to eat. There are many elegant *ristoranti*, particularly in the big cities and resort areas, that serve *nouvelle cuisine* or characteristic dishes whose recipes have been revised and "lightened up" according to the dictates of modern dietetics.

Simpler and more traditional cooking is prepared in an inn-type restaurant often called a *trattoria* or *osteria*. Without any claims to great sophistication, these types of restaurants are usually located on quiet side streets or along small country roads.

And then, of course, found everywhere are pizzerias, customarily open only for dinner, the favorite gathering place of young people and big families and where the specialty is of course pizza, pizza and more pizza in every form imaginable.

(Composition created by chef Antonio Sciullo)

THE MOST TYPICAL PRODUCTS

PASTA

In Italy pasta comes in an infinite number of shapes that can be divided into a number of categories: dried pasta, fresh egg pasta, stuffed pasta, and homemade flour-and-water pasta. We list the most common kinds, many of which are called for in our recipes and you will find illustrated in the photos in that section.

Dried pasta: Bavette, bigoli, bombolotti, bucatini, cannolicchi, capellini, conchiglie, conchiglioni, ditali, eliche, farfalle, fusilli, gnocchetti, maccheroncini, penne, pennette, pici, rigatoni, spaghetti, tonnarelli, tortiglioni, trenette, vermicelli, zite.

Fresh egg pasta: Fettucine, lagane, lasagne, maccheroni (or spaghetti) alla chitarra, pappardelle, tagliatelle, tagliolini.

Fresh stuffed egg pasta: Agnolini, agnolotti, agnolini, cannelloni, cappelletti, pansotti, ravioli, tortelli, tortellini.

Fresh homemade flour-and-water pasta: Cavatelli (or cavatieddi), maccheroni al ferro, orecchiette.

CHEESES

A vast number and variety of cheeses are made in Italy. In fact, it is one of the countries with the greatest number of cheese specialties, some of which are very famous outside Italy too. In many cases these products are named for the place where they are made and belong to a consortium that guarantees their quality and authenticity as well as protecting them against imitations.

The following is a brief list of the best known ones that tells where they are produced. Obviously the list is far from exhaustive since the different regions of Italy produce hundreds of cheeses of various types.

Asiago: Veneto. A semi-fat cheese made from cow's milk. It is light yellow in color and riddled with small holes. There is also a fresh version with a somewhat sweet flavor.

Burrata: Apulia/Campania. This is a fresh cheese from cow's milk which has a smooth white appearance on the outside while inside it contains either butter or a kind of mozzarella, minced and mixed with cream. Hence the flavor is sweet and delicate and very fresh.

Caciocavallo: Southern Italy. Made from cow's milk, this is a hard smooth cheese, light yellow in color. The fresh version is sweet whereas the aged variety is slightly sharp tasting. There is also a smoked version.

Caciotta: Central Italy. These cheeses are quite small, round and flat pieces. They can be made from cow's milk, sheep's milk, or a mixture of the two. They are soft in texture, light in color and are eaten fresh. They can be either delicate or slightly sharp in flavor.

Canestrato: Apulia/Sardinia. Hard and generally made from sheep's milk, this cheese is aged and quite sharp tasting.

Castelmagno: Piedmont. A semi-hard, ivory white cheese that turns dark with aging. The flavor is delicate when young but becomes strong and sharp in the aged variety.

Fiore sardo: Sardinia. Made from sheep's milk, this cheese has a compact texture and is white or light yellow in color. The taste is more or less sharp according to how long it has aged. Besides being eaten alone it is also used for grating.

Fontina: Valle d'Aosta. An elastic cheese made from cow's milk, it is yellow with small holes and quite strong in flavor without being sharp. It is primarily used to make *fonduta* (fondue). See the section on "National Specialties."

Gorgonzola: Lombardy. This is a white cheese streaked with green mold. Made from cow's milk, it is crumbly and has a strong, unique flavor and penetrating odour.

Grana padano: Northeastern Italy. A hard-textured, cow's milk cheese, aged and tasty.
It is mostly used for grating, but is also excellent at the end of a meal. It is delicious in combination with pears.

Mascarpone: Lombardy. This cheese has the consistency of soft butter and is sweet and fat.
It is mostly used for making exquisite pastries or with pasta sauces.

Mozzarella di bufala: Campania. This is a fresh white cheese with a soft, elastic texture that comes in small round shapes. It has a fresh, delicate, slightly sour taste.
The type made from buffalo's milk is softer and more flavorful than the kind made from cow's milk which is produced in all regions.

Parmigiano reggiano: Emilia-Romagna. This is Italy's most famous parmesan cheese, similar to *grana padano* (see above) but more prized. It has a hard, rough texture, a strong flavor, and is mostly used for grating although it is excellent eaten in pieces as an appetizer or to end the meal.

Pecorino: Latium/Sardinia/Tuscany/Sicily. Made from sheep's milk, it is white when fresh and light yellow when aged. The regional varieties differ a little from each other, but they are always hard cheeses with a strong and more or less sharp flavor.

Provolone: Southern Italy and Lombardy. This cheese is semi-hard, smooth, light in color. There is a mild type with a delicate flavor and a sharp variety.

Ricotta: All parts of Italy. This is a fresh, creamy, non-fat cheese made with either sheep's or cow's milk. It is mainly used for pastries or as a filling for fresh egg pasta. In the South there is also an aged kind called *ricotta dura* or *ricotta salata* which is fairly sharp and is usually used for grating.

Robiola: Piedmont and Lombardy. A fresh, creamy, white cheese, ideal for spreading on bread.

Stracchino: Lombardy. Fresh, soft, and white with a delicate flavor, it is also known as *crescenza*.

Taleggio: Lombardy. A fat, light-colored cheese made from cow's milk, it has a soft, buttery texture and a slightly sour taste.

COLD CUT MEATS

There is no Italian region which does not boast a long tradition of specialties made from pork and there is a wealth of products coming from this industry. Some regions produce not only prized pork products but cold cuts from other meats as well.

Boar hams are just one example. Many of these products are also very famous outside Italy, but there are many others, less famous, that certainly are worth tasting when available.

Bresaola: Lombardy. Very lean cured beef, shaped like a large *salame* with a uniform dark red color. It can be aged to various degrees and is usually eaten as an appetizer, thinly sliced and dressed with oil, lemon, and pepper.

Cacciatorini: Small *salame* of not very finely ground meat. It is aged and very tasty but not sharp. Found all over Italy.

Capocollo: In southern and central Italy this is the name given to a dark red *salame* veined with fat. In the North it is called *coppa*.

Coppa (1): Emilia-Romagna. An aged *salame*, mostly lean but with veins of fat. Particularly appreciated is the product made in the region around Piacenza. It is generally eaten as an appetizer together with other cured meats or as a country-style snack with bread.

Coppa (2): Central Italy. A very different product from its namesake in Emilia-Romagna. It is made from the more humble parts of the pig (head, snout, etc.), cooked with herbs and vegetables, then allowed to cool, and then pressed. It is usually eaten in a salad with olives, celery, etc. and makes a very tasty appetizer.

Cotechino: Made in a casing and eaten cooked, this is a mixture of pork, lard, and pigskin. It is eaten almost exclusively in winter, and in that season makes part of the "mixed boiled meats" dish in north Italy.

Culatello: A much-prized Parma specialty that is made from pig's leg. It is lean and aged but tender, mild and tasty.

Finocchiona: Tuscan *salame* with a soft texture and seasoned with fennel seeds and garlic.

Fiocchetto: This too is a Parma specialty taken from pig's leg like the more prized *culatello*. Lean with veins of fat, it seems similar to *coppa* (1) but is milder tasting, less spicy.

Mortadella: Produced everywhere, but especially good in the Bologna region. It is a very big *salume* (cold cut) indeed, with rosy flesh into which many little cubes of lard are added. Aromatic and with a distinct flavor, it is seasoned with pepper and, sometimes, pistachio nuts.

Prosciutto crudo: One of the most famous Italian gastronomical products, taken from pig's leg, salted, left to age, and eaten raw. This ham can be soft and mild or harder and more savory. In either case it is one of the best appetizers when combined with fruit such as cantaloup or figs. The finest kinds are the *San Daniele*, produced in the town of that name in Friuli, and that of Parma. Both of these are soft and mild.

Salame: A cased sausage which can be finely or coarsely ground, but always contains a lot of fat. There are many different types, but one particularly notes: *Felino salami* (Emilia-Romagna); *Varzi*, seasoned with garlic; *Ferrara* (Emilia-Romagna), with a strong garlic flavor; the *salamin d'la duja* (Piedmont), which is preserved in lard; *Milanese*, finely and homogeneously ground; *Secondigliano* (Campania), spiced with hot red chili peppers.

Soppressa: Veneto. A rather coarsely ground kind of *salame*.

Soppressata: Central and southern Italy. An oval rather than round *salame*. The most famous version is that of

Fabriano (Marches) with small cubes of fat.

Speck: Tridentine-South Tyrol. Smoked raw ham, very lean but surrounded with a ring of fat.

Zampone: Emilia-Romagna. A *salame* eaten cooked, very tasty and similar to *cotechino*, traditionally eaten on New Year's Eve with lentils.

OIL

The most prized kind of oil is extra-virgin olive oil, which is obtained from the first crushing of the olives. It is the most flavorful and the best for using uncooked.
The principal kinds vary according to the zone of production.

Gardesano: Produced around Lake Garda, it is very light and delicate in flavor, most suitable for use with vegetables and freshwater fish.

Ligurian: Light in color and delicate tasting, it is particularly good with fish.

Tuscan: With its more intense color and flavor, it is excellent with vegetables and meat.

Umbrian: It is similar to Tuscan oil with a deeper color and a slightly bitter aftertaste.

Latium: A heavy body and intense color verging on dark green. It is excellent on *bruschetta* (see "Appetizers") when of good quality.

Apulian: Very flavorful, rather heavy, intense in color.

SWEETS AND PASTRIES

When it comes to sweets and pastries, each region of Italy boasts its numerous specialties, above all cookies and biscuits. Here we list some of these products.

Amaretti: These are very light almond cookies, made with sugar and egg white, that have that special almond flavor. Particularly prized are the ones coming from Saronno in Lombardy and the Sardinian ones.

Cannoli: These Sicilian pastries are on the top of the list of Italian pastries. A crunchy pastry crust conceals an aromatic *ricotta* cream.

Confetti: The best *confetti* in the world are made in the town of Sulmona in the central Italian region of the Abruzzo.
Besides the common white *confetti* there are an infinite number of other forms and colors which are used to concoct fanciful compositions (bouquets of flowers, butterflies, etc.)

Fichi in crocetta: These dried figs are a Calabrian specialty. They are joined together on wooden skewers and filled with almonds or walnuts.

Frutti di marzapane (Marzipan fruits): These marzipan (almond paste) sweets are typically Sicilian and are modeled into very realistic looking fruits.

Gelati: Italian ice cream is famous throughout the world. If you ever visit Italy we advise you to try it in the big ice cream parlors, particularly those which have a sign indicating that they make their own products. These shops, besides offering homemade specialties, have a wide selection of flavors, from the most traditional ones to the most original.

Gianduiotti: These delicious chocolates come originally from Turin but are to be found everywhere. They have a nutty taste. The traditional shape is triangular and they are wrapped in gold paper.

Granita: This very refreshing specialty is made of shaved ice mixed with coffee, mint or fruit syrups and is delightful in summer. The Sicilian ones are especially good.

Panforte: A Siennese specialty, the round, flat *panforte* is made of dried and candied fruits mixed with honey and spices.

Paste: The pastry shops in central and southern Italy offer a particularly wide selection of pastries and cookies, from cream puffs in many flavors to Sicilian *cannoli*, and so on. On holidays and weekends especially Italians make sure to take home a selection of delicious assorted pastries.

Sfogliatelle ricce: Almost all pastry shops in Italy have these Neapolitan pastries which are of course better in Naples than anywhere else. They are made of a very thin, crunchy puff pastry filled with a soft cream of *ricotta* and candied fruits.

Spongata: Similar to the *panforte* of Siena, this is a specialty of Emilia and certain parts of Lombardy and is to be found almost exclusively during the Christmas season.

Torrone: A long, rectangular-shaped candy made of almonds or pecans, egg whites, and sugar. The most typical ones come from Cremona in Lombardy, the Abruzzi, or Sicily, though they are produced in just about every part of Italy. Some kinds are covered with chocolate. Torrone is most easily found during the Christmas season.

WINES

As everyone knows, Italy is one of the world's greatest wine producing countries. Hundreds of different types are available, whites, rosés, reds, and dessert wines. To describe and name them all would require an entire book in itself. Thus we must limit ourselves to brief descriptions of the most popular ones, specifying the areas from which they come.

Aglianico del Vulture: Basilicata. Dry red suitable with red meat.

Albana: Emilia-Romagna. White. Comes in both dry and fruity versions with an alcoholic content of about 12%.

Alcamo: Sicily. White, dry, fruity.

Aleatico: Apulia. Red, sweet, intense, about 15%; there is also a dessert version of about 18% alcoholic content.

Amarone: Veneto. A heavy red with an intense flavor, very suitable for red meat roasts.

Asti spumante: Piedmont. One of the best known Italian sparkling wines. Sweet and aromatic, very suitable for dessert.

Barabaresco: Piedmont. Red, dry, robust. Slightly aged. About 12% alcoholic content.

Barbera: Piedmont. Red, dry, intense.

Bardolino: Veneto. Ruby red, dry, slightly bitter

Barolo: Piedmont. One of the noblest Italian wines. Red, dry, robust.

Bianco di Pitigliano: Tuscany. White, dry, slightly bitter.

Brunello di Montalcino: Tuscany. Another very great wine, among the choicest. Red, intense, dry, aged at least four years.

Cabernet: Tridentine, South Tyrol, Friuli, Veneto. Red and dry. Comes in different qualities.

Cannonau: Sardinia. Red and dry or fruity according to the type.

Capri: Isle of Capri. White, it is fresh and dry tasting. There is also a red version.

Castel del Monte: Apulia. There are three types; white (fresh and dry), rosé (dry, harmonious), and red.

Castelli Romani: Latium. White, red, or rosé. The best known is the white, which is good throughout the meal.

Chianti: Tuscany. Probably the most famous Italian wine. Red, dry, intense, it is suitable with hearty meat dishes.

Cinque Terre: Liguria. White and dry. There is a syrupy, sweet dessert type called **Sciacchetrà**.

Cirò: Calabria. Red, white and rosé types. In all cases it is a dry, harmonious wine.

Colli Albani: Latium. White, dry, delicate, fruity.

Colli Berici: Veneto. A name given to a variety of wines, some of which are white, dry and delicate, and others hearty dry reds.

Colli Euganei: Veneto. Exists in red and white versions which can be either dry or fruity or a muscatel (sweet).

Colli Lanuvini: Latium. White, dry and delicate.

Colli del Trasimeno: Umbria. White (harmonious, delicate) or red (dry).

Collio: Friuli. A name for a variety of wines, some white and dry, others red, hearty and aromatic.

Dolcetto: Piedmont. There are a number of kinds that take their names from the regions where they are produced. They are all red, dry and slightly bitter despite the name.

Erbaluce di Caluso: Piedmont. White. There is also the

Caluso Passito, a sweet dessert wine.

Est! Est! Est!: Latium. White and dry, full bodied.

Falerio: Marches. White, dry, slightly sour.

Frascati: Latium. White, dry, delicate. There is also a sparkling type and a sweet one, **Cannellino**.

Gattinara: Piedmont. Red, dry, slightly bitter, aged at least four years.

Greco di Tufo: Campania. White, dry, delicate. Comes in a sparkling version too.

Grignolino: Piedmont. Red, dry, pleasantly bitter.

Lambrusco: Emilia-Romagna. Red, fizzy, light. Comes in dry and fruity types.

Locorotondo: Apulia. White, dry, delicate. There is alsosparkling type.

Malvasia: Various regions. A sweet, aromatic dessert wine.

Marino: Latium. White, dry, fruity.

Martina Franca: Apulia. White, dry, delicate. Also comes in a sparkling version.

Marsala: Sicily. A heavy dessert wine with a high

alcoholic content. It can be either sweet or dry. In both cases the flavor is strong and full.

Merlot: Various regions. Red with a full, aromatic taste. Sometimes slightly bitter.

Moscato (Muscatel): Various regions. A white dessert wine, sweet and delicate, sometimes fizzy.
There are also richer versions with a higher alcoholic content.

Nebbiolo: Piedmont. Red, dry, lots of body, about 12% alcoholic content.

Nuragus: Sardinia. White, dry, slightly sour.

Oltrepò Pavese: Lombardy. A name for a number of wines among which one should note the **Bonarda** (red and fresh tasting) and the **Riesling** (white, dry).

Orvieto: Umbria. White with dry and fruity types.

Pinot: Friuli and other regions. One of the most popular wines in Italy, it exists in the "white," "gray," and "black" types. There is also a sparkling version.

Prosecco di Valdobbiadene: Veneto. White and either dry or fruity. Sparkling types are also available.

Sangiovese: Romagna. Red, dry, with a bitterish aftertaste.

Soave: Veneto. Dry and white. Medium body.

Spumante: It is the equivalent of French champagne, if less prized. But a number of types have really little to envy of their more famous French brothers. There are also some sweet kinds. They are usually served at the end of the meal, but are also good as aperitifs or even during the meal.

Teraldego: Tridentine-South Tyrol. A dry, fruity red with a slight almond flavor, or a rosé which has less body.

Trebbiano: Romagna. A dry white which also exists in a dry or sweet sparkling version.

Valpolicella: Veneto. Red, full-bodied, dry or slightly sweet.

Verdicchio di Jesi: Marches. Dry and white with a slight bitter aftertaste.

Vermentino di Gallura: Sardinia. White, dry and slightly bitter.

Vernaccia: Tuscany. White, dry, fresh, bitterish.

Vino nobile di Montepulciano: Tuscany. Red, dry, intense, aged at least two years.

Vin santo: Tuscany. A heavy dessert wine. Good with dry sweet biscuits.

LIQUEURS

It is inevitable that a country which produces not only wines but much fruit and aromatic herbs should have a long tradition of liqueurs and distilled spirits. Particular emphasis must be given to the many bitter liqueurs, very aromatic digestive liqueurs made from herbs, spices, or citrus peels. **Grappa**, which is made primarily in Tridentine, Veneto, and Friuli, comes in a variety of types some of which are flavored with fruit. Also, in restaurants in Italy a house liqueur or bitter is often available which is made by the proprietors of family-run restaurants.

Amaretto di Saronno: Very sweet with the aroma of almonds, it is produced on an industrial scale.

Aurum: A sweet orange liqueur, it is not extremely common, but has a very pleasant bouquet. Often used to flavor pastries, it is also excellent straight or on the rocks.

Centerbe: A very strong and aromatic digestive liqueur with a high alcoholic content, this is among the liqueurs known as bitters (*amari*) and comes from the Abruzzo.

Grappa: A highly alcoholic distilled spirit, that is produced both industrially and locally. In the second case one finds varieties with different aromas in mountain regions. Among these a blueberry grappa is particularly good.

Limoncino (or **Limoncello**): A sweet and very aromatic lemon liqueur, it is typical of Campania, the Amalfi coast area in particular. It should be drunk with ice.

Mirto: A Sardinian liqueur which has a strong aroma of the myrtle plant for which it is named.

Nocino: A digestive liqueur made by infusing green walnuts in alcohol, it is strong and concentrated, somewhat sweet and typical of Emilia-Romagna.

Sambuca: This liqueur, which has an intense aroma of anise, is produced industrially. In Rome it is common to drink it with "a fly" in it, which is to say, a coffee bean.

Sassolino: This too is an anise-flavored liqueur from the region around Modena, sweet and often used in pastries. But it is not easy to find outside of its native area.

Strega: A sweet and aromatic liqueur from Campania, but found everywhere since it is produced industrially. It is excellent poured over ice cream.

Vermouth: This is not a true liqueur but rather a special wine-flavored one with aromatic herbs that comes from Piedmont. It is served as an aperitif or in cocktails.

OTHER SPECIALTIES

There are many other excellent products worth keeping in mind besides those already mentioned (wines, oils, cold cut meats). In this case too, we cannot claim to be exhaustive, but can only attempt to indicate the most important ones.

Aceto aromatico (Aromatic vinegar): A specialty of Modena, this is a very prized vinegar that is suitable to season many different dishes.

Bottarga (Fish roe): This is a mixture of the roe of various fishes, usually mullet, which is pressed, salted and left to age for a few months. It has the form of a square *salame* and is usually eaten on toasted bread, as an appetizer, cut into thin slices and dressed with lemon and oil. It is often used for a pasta condiment. There are also types made from the roe of tuna, but these are stronger in flavor and less choice. *Bottarga* is a Sardinian specialty. If well conserved, it will keep for several months in the refrigerator.

Caffè: As everyone knows, the Italians have a weakness for coffee which they usually drink made in the espresso way, very concentrated and with a little reddish brown foam on the surface. Then too, in Italy one finds excellent blends of coffee suitable for being used in the Italian household coffee maker, the moka. In general, we more readily find dark roasted coffee beans (which are more bitter and aromatic) in the South, whereas in the North they are roasted less and are lighter in color. Naturally, real connoisseurs demand that the coffee be ground only just before it is made so that it doesn't lose its aroma. It is also often used to make creams, desserts and ice cream.

Ciccioli: These are small pieces of fried pork fat, rather hard to digest, but very savory. They can be eaten as an appetizer or used in savory pies. They are generally made in autumn and spring.

Focaccia: This is the name in several regions for a kind of very soft plain pizza with a generous amount of oil poured over it.

Grissini: Thin, dry, crunchy breadsticks. There are various types and sizes which the best-stocked bakery shops in Italy carry. There is also a vast production of industrial products often found in Italian restaurants where they are served along with bread.

Mostarda: A specialty of Veneto and Lombardy (particularly Cremona), this is a very special condiment for boiled meats consisting of fruit treated with syrups and

mustard which give it a characteristic sweet-sharp taste. Today it is primarily produced industrially and so can be found in grocery shops everywhere.

Piadina: A typical pizza of Romagna which is generally filled with cold cuts and served hot. Outside Romagna, an industrial type can be found but which is not on the same level as that made in its native territory.

Porchetta: This is pork sliced from the whole roasted animal and strongly seasoned with garlic and aromatic herbs. It is available in Umbria, but most of all in Latium at markets and by street vendors. Often served as hearty sandwiches.

Tartufi (Truffles): There are two principal areas that produce this aromatic tuber: around Alba in Piedmont, and near Norcia in Umbria, where the black kind is much more common. They are found during a rather limited period in late autumn.

Conserved in oil or in other ways, they can also be bought during the rest of the year, but they have less aroma. Being very rare and prized items, their cost is naturally high, especially the white ones.

RECIPES

Acciughe marinate

APPETIZERS

Although appetizers (*antipasti*) are not usually served at family meals (with the possible exception of Sundays and holidays) they are essential at formal dinner parties. Restaurants too always offer a varied choice. In recent years many have adopted the system of offering a buffet where the customer can help himself to greens, cold cuts, cheeses, and several other dishes, such as marinated seafood salad.

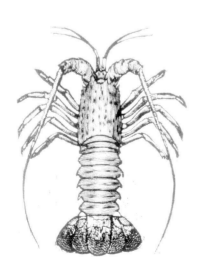

Acciughe marinate
(Marinated anchovies)

This dish can be served by itself, but more often it is part of mixed appetizers: olives, pickled vegetables and those preserved in oil eaten with bread. It is native to the southern coastal regions.
One variant consists in marinating the anchovies in vinegar rather than lemon juice, but the recipe we offer has a more delicate flavor.

Ingredients *(For 4) :*
Fresh anchovies   1 lb (500 g)
6 juicy lemons
Parsley, garlic, hot red peppers,
*   extra-virgin olive oil, salt*

Preparation:
Clean the anchovies removing the innards and heads. Slice the fish open and remove the backbones.
Cut off the tails then rinse and dry.

Put the fish close together into a non-metal container in a single layer with their bellies up. Salt them lightly and pour on the strained juice of 3 lemons. Cover the container with wrapper and keep in a cool place for 2-3 hours, then drain off the juice. Next, season the fish with the crushed pieces of a dried red pepper, 2 thinly sliced garlic cloves, minced parsley, and the juice of the remaining 3 lemons. Cover again with plastic wrapper and keep in the refrigerator for 8-12 hours.
When serving, drain off the juice and add a drop of oil.

Antipasto misto
ALL'ITALIANA
(Mixed Italian appetizers)

This dish, an assortment of the simplest and most traditional of appetizers in all parts of Italy, is often served on Sundays and holidays.

34

Antipasto misto all'italiana

There is no restaurant where you cannot ask for it.

Its ingredients (salami, *mixed pickles, olives, and sometimes cheese) varies from region to region only in that the most popular local products are used. The recipe that follows is the one most easily found in restaurants.*

Bread and Italian red wine generally accompany it. A famous variant of this is the classic summer hors-d'oeuvre of prosciutto e melone *where cured Parma or San Daniele ham is served with slices of fresh, sweet, juicy cantaloup, or else,* salame e fichi *which is the same concept of combining cured meats with a very sweet summer fruit, figs.*

Ingredients *(For 4) :*

Cured Parma ham	*4 slices*
Thick salami	*4 slices*
Piacenza coppa	*4 slices*
Cooked ham	*4 slices*
Parmesan cheese	*7 oz (200 g)*
Mixed pickles	*4 oz (120 g)*
Green olives	*4 oz (100 g)*
2 hard-boiled eggs	

Preparation:

Arrange the sliced cold cuts on a serving plate leaving the center free for the olives and mixed pickles. Cut the cheese into fairly thick pieces and place these on the cold cuts. Garnish with wedges of hard-boiled egg and, if you like, fresh tomato.

If you cannot find...

The cold cuts mentioned, use any others... as long as they are Italian!

ARANCINI DI RISO
(Rice croquettes)

This is a typical Sicilian dish. There are regional differences with regard to the filling of the croquettes (sometimes you will find them with chopped cooked mushrooms), but the basic dish remains the same. The croquettes can be served as an appetizer or as a first course in place of pasta, but in Sicily they are generally eaten as a snack.

Ingredients *(For 4) :*

Rice	*7 oz*	*(200 g)*
Ground beef	*5 oz*	*(150 g)*
Cooked peas	*3 oz*	*(70 g)*
Mozzarella	*3 oz*	*(80 g)*

2 eggs

A small onion, packet of saffron, tomato paste, olive oil, breadcrumbs, grated parmesan, flour, dry white wine, seed oil, salt, pepper

Preparation:

Mince the onion and brown it in 2 tablespoons of oil. After a few minutes add the ground beef and let it turn color. Next add salt and pepper, a glass of wine and, when this evaporates, 2 tablespoons of tomato paste dissolved in a little hot water. Cook the meat on a low flame for about an hour. Then add the peas and turn off the fire.

Boil the rice in salted water and drain when it is *al dente* (that is, completely cooked but still firm). Let it cool, then add an egg, the saffron and three tablespoons of grated parmesan. With flour on your hands, roll the rice into balls a little larger than an egg, squash them flat, and in the cavity thus formed place a little of the meat sauce and a cube of mozzarella. Close up the rice ball, roll it in flour, then in beaten egg, and finally in breadcrumbs. Fry the croquettes in abundant seed oil. When they are golden, take them out, put them on some paper to absorb the oil, and serve at once.

Bagna cauda

This sauce with its very strong flavor is one of the most traditional items of Piedmontese cuisine. It is used as a dip with raw vegetables and makes a fun and mouth-watering opener for any meal.

Ingredients *(For 4) :*

Cream   *7 oz (200 g)*
6 salted anchovies
4-6 cloves garlic
4 very fresh artichokes
2 sweet bell peppers
One celery heart, olive oil, salt

Preparation:
Mince the garlic and put it in a pot with a cup of oil. Heat until the garlic begins to turn color, then remove from the heat. Add the anchovies that have been washed, boned, and cut into small pieces. Let them dissolve in the hot oil then add the cream and heat the sauce without letting it boil. Correct the salt if needed and pour the sauce into 4 small bowls. In the meantime you should have cleaned all the vegetables and removed the hardest parts. Cut them into pieces and serve with the sauce.

Bruschetta
(Italian toast)

This is one of the simplest and most popular Italian appetizers. Three central Italian regions – Latium, Tuscany, and Umbria – make claim to originating this dish, but certainly it is most common in Latium. There two versions are offered: alongside the simpler and more traditional one, restaurants and pizzerias offer another one with fresh tomato (Bruschetta al pomodoro). We will describe. A word of advice: if you cannot get extra-virgin

Bruschetta al pomodoro

olive oil, do not attempt to make bruschetta!

Ingredients (For 4) :
Fresh home-style bread
  (pane casareccio)   *4 slices*
Extra-virgin olive oil, oregano, garlic,
  salt, pepper
Optional: chopped fresh tomatoes

Preparation:
For the tomato version, chop the tomatoes into small pieces after having removed their seeds and drained them. Put them into a bowl with 2 sliced garlic cloves, salt, and a few spoons of oil. You can also add a little fresh basil if you like. Macerate for at least an hour to blend the flavors.
Toast the bread lightly in the oven and season it with oil, salt, pepper, and oregano or else with the tomato mixture. Serve at once.

CALZONI

A close relative of pizza, calzoni originate in Campania, but by now they are to be found in any Italian rosticceria *or* pizzeria. *Generally they are eaten between meals as snacks, but they can also be eaten as appetizers or in place of pasta courses. The traditional filling is the one we give in this recipe. Under the name of* panzerotti *and with a filling of tomato and mozzarella or greens, it is a typical dish in Apulia and other parts of southern Italy.*

Ingredients (For 4) :

Flour	*11 oz*	*(300 g)*
Brewer's yeast	*1/3 oz*	*(15 g)*
Sausage	*7 oz*	*(200 g)*
Mozzarella	*7 oz*	*(200 g)*
Ricotta	*6 oz*	*(200 g)*
Oil, salt, pepper		

Preparation:
Make the dough as indicated in the recipe for *Pizza Margherita* in this section. For the filling, break the sausage into small bits and then brown in a pan. When it has turned color, pour off its grease and mix in the *ricotta*, the minced mozzarella, salt and pepper. Cut eight disks out of the pizza dough and put some filling on each one. Fold each in half and press the edges firmly closed.
Deep fry the *calzoni* in boiling oil until golden, or cook them in an oven pre-heated to 450° F (230°C) for about twenty minutes after having brushed them with oil.

CARPACCIO

This dish was invented by a Venetian bar-owner in the fifties. Despite its short history it has already had such great success that it can be found throughout Italy.
There are many variations, but the most popular is the simplest one, which we give here, and those versions which add raw sliced mushrooms or rucola *(a highly aromatic kind of green salad leaf).*

Ingredients (For 4) :

Very lean fillet of beef	*1/2 lb*	*(250 g)*
Parmesan cheese	*3 oz*	*(80 g)*
A lemon, salt, pepper, extra-virgin olive oil		

Carpaccio

Preparation:
Have the butcher cut the fillet into very thin slices. Place these on plates in single layers. Beat 4 tablespoons of oil with the lemon juice and a pinch of salt and pepper. Pour onto the sliced fillets and let them rest for 15 minutes. Place thinly cut parmesan on the meat and serve. If you like, you can also add thinly sliced and very fresh raw mushrooms, or broken *rucola* leaves, or sliced raw artichoke hearts.

Cocktail di scampi
(Scampi cocktail)

Ingredients *(For 4) :*
Scampi tails   14 oz (400 g)
A celery heart, lettuce, mayonnaise, brandy, ketchup, cream, bay leaf, parsley, celery, salt, pepper, lemon, white wine, black olives and a few shrimp for decoration.

Preparation:
Boil a slice of lemon, a few sprigs of parsley, salt, peppercorns, a bay leaf, and half a glass of wine in some water.

Cocktail di scampi

Crostini alla romana
(Roman toast)

*As the name indicates this is a
specialty found in Roman trattorie and
pizzerias. It is prepared quickly and
easily and requires only a few simple
ingredients.*

Ingredients *(For 4):*
French "baguette"
  type bread   12 slices
Mozzarella   12 slices
6-8 anchovy fillets in oil
Butter   4 oz (100 g)

Preparation:
Toast the bread in the oven for a few
minutes. Meanwhile fry the anchovies
in the butter until they dissolve. Put a
slice of mozzarella on each piece of
toast, then return to the oven for about
a minute, until the mozzarella is half
melted.
Take the *crostini* out of the oven, pour
on the anchovy sauce, and serve at once,
adding, if you like, a bit of parsley.

After it has boiled for 20 minutes add
the shelled scampi tails and cook for
2-3 minutes. Drain well.
In a salad bowl mix the scampi with a
sliced celery heart and 5-6 lettuce
leaves cut into strips. Salt lightly. Mix
3 tablespoons of mayonnaise with one
of brandy, one of cream and one of
tomato ketchup. Salt and pepper the
sauce lightly.
Place four pretty lettuce leaves in four
glass cocktail cups (or a large serving
dish), then the scampi, and pour on the
sauce.
Garnish with the black olives and the
shrimps. Serve chilled.

CROSTINI AL PROSCIUTTO
(Cured ham on toast)

This recipe also originates in Latium, in fact in Rome. It too is a very quickly prepared appetizer, and very savory. If you cannot find the ingredients indicated, you can use others which will make an equally tasty appetizer, but you will not be able to say it is typically Italian.

Ingredients *(For 4)* :

French "baguette" type bread	*12 slices*
Cured ham (prosciutto)	*6 slices*
Mozzarella	*12 slices*
Oil	

Preparation:

Brush a little oil on the bread slices and toast them in the oven for several minutes. Then cover them with a slice of ham and a slice of mozzarella. Pour another bit of oil on each slice and return to the oven for 1-2 minutes more, just enough for the mozzarella to begin melting. Serve at once.

If you cannot find...
Prosciutto: substitute cooked ham.
Mozzarella: substitute another soft melting cheese with a rather delicate flavor.

CROSTINI TOSCANI
(Tuscan toast)

This is very popular in Tuscany, where it is the most typical of all appetizers. The restaurant which does not offer it simply doesn't exist!
To remain most faithful to the original

Crostini toscani

recipe one must use Tuscan bread, which is made without salt and thus is best suited to the very savory garnishing.
As an alternative to chicken livers the original recipe also allows the use of spleen, but this ingredient is harder to find, at least outside of Tuscany.

Ingredients *(For 4) :*
French "baguette"
  type bread   *12 slices*
Chicken livers   *5 oz (150 g)*
2 anchovy fillets in oil
A small onion, parsley,
  breadcrumbs, dry Marsala wine,
  olive oil, salt, pepper

Preparation:
Mince the onion very finely and brown in a pan with 3 tablespoons of oil. Then add the chicken livers, cleaned and chopped small and cook on a medium flame for about 10 minutes. Sprinkle on 2 tablespoons of Marsala and let it evaporate almost entirely. Put the chicken livers and anchovies through the blender. Add a spoonful of breadcrumbs, a little minced parsley, salt and pepper. Mix well and spread on slices of lightly toasted bread. Serve at once.

If you cannot find...
Marsala wine: substitute dry red wine or even a spoonful of vinegar.

Erbazzone

This is a typical savory pie from Emilia-Romagna.
Cut into slices it can serve as a snack as well as an hors-d'œuvre, or to accompany aperitifs.

Ingredients *(For 4) :*
Fresh spinach   approx. 2 lb   (1 kg)
Beet greens   *2 lb   (1 kg)*
Flour   *2 heaping cups (300 g)*
2 eggs
Parmesan cheese, half an onion,
  garlic, parsley, milk, butter, seed oil,
  salt

Preparation:
Make a dough with the flour, a pinch of salt, 2 tablespoons of oil, and as much milk as needed, about half a glass, to obtain a firm and elastic dough. Cover this dough with a cloth while you make the filling.
Wash the spinach and beet greens and cook them with only a pinch of salt (no water). When cooked, press out the water and mince finely.
Mince the onion and brown in 2 ounces (50 grams) of butter. Then add the greens and let the flavors blend for several minutes. Add minced garlic and parsley and, once you remove this mixture from the fire, 2 tablespoons of parmesan, and the eggs. Correct the salt.
Butter a large oven dish and line it with a good half of the dough that you have rolled out into a very thin sheet. Put in the filling, spread it level, and cover the pie with the remaining dough, pinching it together with the dough underneath.
Prick some holes in the top crust and brush on a little oil. Bake the pie in an oven pre-heated to 400°F (220° to 230°C) until it has turned golden above and below. Best served tepid or cold.

If you cannot find...
Parmesan cheese: substitute another tasty cheese that can be grated.

Fiori di zucchine ripieni
(Stuffed zucchini flowers)

At the beginning of summer, the delicate zucchini flowers begin appearing on Italian tables. The simplest preparation is to dip them in a batter of flour, water and salt, and fry them in oil. Our recipe is a bit less basic but particularly savory. It is native to Latium, even if it can be found in other parts of the country with a different filling. For example, in Liguria it is customary to stuff the flowers with dried mushrooms.

Ingredients *(For 4) :*
16 very fresh zucchini flowers
Mozzarella   4 1/2 oz (120 g)
5-6 anchovy fillets in oil
One egg, flour, salt, pepper, seed oil

Preparation:
Wash the flowers carefully and remove their pistils. Dry them on a paper towel. Put a strip of mozzarella and a piece of anchovy into each flower. Bend the points of the flowers inwards so that the filling remains inside. Beat the egg with very little salt, pepper, and a few tablespoons of flour. You should get a semi-liquid batter without lumps.

Dip in the flowers and fry in abundant, very hot oil on a medium flame until they turn golden. Leave for a moment on paper to absorb the oil and serve very hot, sprinkled with a little salt.

If you cannot find...
Mozzarella: use a melting cheese, like

Fiori di zucchine

Swiss cheese, but in this case it is better to substitute cooked ham for the anchovies. Mozzarella is the only cheese that blends well with anchovies.

Fonduta
(Fondue)

This dish is a typical Piedmontese specialty, even if it probably originates in Swiss-French cuisine. The clue to its regional tie is the use of one of Italy's most famous cheeses (fontina) produced in the Val d'Aosta, and of white truffle which, in Italy, grows only around Alba, a Piedmontese small town.

Ingredients *(For 4) :*

Fontina *cheese*	*10 oz*	*(300 g)*
Milk	*approx. 1 pt (1 ¹/₂ liters)*	
Butter	*1 oz*	*(25 g)*

3 egg yolks
French "baguette" type bread, salt, a small white truffle

Preparation:

Cut the *fontina* in slices and soak in the milk for a few hours.

Melt the butter in a double boiler, add the *fontina* with 2-3 tablespoons of milk and melt it slowly stirring constantly with a whisk. When you have obtained a smooth cream add the egg yolks one at a time.

Add salt to taste and put the fondue in a suitable dish where it will keep warm.

Slice very thin slices of white truffle over the top and serve with bread cubes which each guest will dip into the cheese mixture.

If you cannot find...

Fontina: you can use a cheese such as *gruyere*, but in that case your fondue will be Swiss rather than Italian! White truffle: use black truffle or simply white pepper.

Gatò di patate
(Potato cake)

The name is an "Italianization" of the French word gâteau, *and in fact the dish was introduced in Naples during the last century under the Bourbon domination, a dynasty of French origin. With the addition of other ingredients it can also be found in other regions and under other names. What we offer here is the traditional Campania recipe. In any case, it is a dish that can make a one-plate meal.*

Ingredients *(For 4) :*

Floury potatoes	*2 lb*	*(1 kg)*
Spicy salame	*4 oz*	*(100 g)*
Mozzarella	*7 oz*	*(200 g)*

5 eggs
Parmesan cheese, breadcrumbs, milk, butter, salt, pepper

Preparation:

Boil the potatoes in their jackets for 40 minutes, peel and mash. To this puree add 4 tablespoons of grated parmesan cheese, 2 eggs, about half a glass of milk, salt, pepper, and the

salami cut into small cubes.
Hard boil the remaining eggs and slice. Butter a baking dish and line with breadcrumbs, then spread in the potato mixture. Add the slices of mozzarella and the eggs. Add salt, pepper, and cover with the remaining potato mixture.
Sprinkle some breadcrumbs over the top and very thin slices of butter, then bake for 20 minutes in a 425° F (200° C) oven.

If you cannot find...
Spicy *salame*: use another kind of *salame* or smoked bacon.
Mozzarella: use a melting cheese.
Parmesan: you can use any other savory grating cheese.

IMPEPATA DI COZZE
(Peppered mussels)

This appetizer is also known as sauté di cozze *and comes from Campania, although it is also common in Latium and other coastal regions with little variation. A very simple way of cooking mussels, it is essential for them to be very fresh.*

Impepata di cozze

Ingredients *(For 4) :*
Mussels   3 lb (1¹/₂ kg)
Olive oil, parsley, salt, pepper

Preparation:
Brush the mussels clean under running water and then soak them in salted cold water for several hours, changing the water a few times.
In one (or better two) large pans, heat

about half a glass of oil, put in the mussels, cover and cook on a high flame for a few minutes until all the mussels have opened.

Then add salt if necessary, minced parsley, and a lot of pepper. Serve them in their broth with bread or preferably toast.

INSALATA CAPRESE
(Capri salad)

Better known simply as caprese, *this dish is very simple and fresh tasting. It is often offered in the summer as a main course or a one-course meal. In its most typical and tasty version mozzarella made from buffalo's milk is used, which is produced in Campania. But more commonly the mozzarella is made from cow's milk. This is less desirable but easier to find.*

Ingredients *(For 4) :*
Mozzarella   14 oz (400 g)
4 ripe tomatoes
Extra-virgin olive oil, fresh basil, salt, pepper

Insalata caprese

Preparation:

Cut the mozzarella into slices and wash the tomatoes. Cut the latter in half and remove the seeds. Then cut them into wedges and alternate with slices of mozzarella on the serving plate. Dress with salt, pepper, and oil, then sprinkle with broken fresh basil leaves. Let the dish sit for about 20 minutes before serving.

INSALATA DI MARE
(Seafood salad)

No seafood restaurant would think of leaving this dish off its menu. This appetizer is truly excellent only when made with the freshest of ingredients (whereas it is sometimes made with frozen ones). It can be embellished with shrimp, mussels and other molluscs, or even with tiny pieces of sweet red peppers, but the recipe we give here is the most traditional one.

Ingredients *(For 4)* :
A small octopus approx. 11 oz (300 g)
Small polyps   1¹/₂ lb (500 g)

A small squid   11 oz (300 g)
Garlic, parsley, salt, one lemon, extra-virgin olive oil

Preparation:

Clean all the seafood and cook in slightly salted cold water (possibly together with onion, celery, and parsley seasoning). The octopus will need about half an hour, so the polyps and squid should be added when it is half cooked. Allow the seafood to cool in its water, then cut into small pieces. Mix 5-6 tablespoons of oil with the strained juice of half a lemon, a minced garlic clove, and salt. Let it sit for half an hour then strain and pour over the seafood. Macerate for another 10-15 minutes in a cool place before serving. Sprinkle with parsley.

Insalata di mare

Involtini di melanzane
(Eggplant rolls)

There are a number of versions of this tasty appetizer that comes from southern Italy.
They differ mainly in the filling, and use of tomato sauce, as in this recipe. The rolls can also be made with bell peppers which have first been roasted under the grill and then carefully peeled.

Ingredients *(For 4)* :

Eggplant	*1 lb (500 g)*
Tomato pulp	*14 oz (400 g)*
Mozzarella	*4 oz (100 g)*
Breadcrumbs,	

Parsley, salt, garlic, fresh basil, hot red peppers, parmesan, olive oil

Preparation:
Peel the eggplant and cut into rather thin strips.
Make layers of these strips on an inclined cutting board and salt each layer and let them sit for an hour to draw out the water, then rinse and dry. Fry in abundant oil until the eggplant becomes soft but not dry.
As the strips finish cooking take them out and lay them on paper to absorb the oil.
Prepare the tomato sauce: brown a garlic clove in 2 tablespoons of oil and remove it when golden.
Add the tomato, salt, a few basil leaves and let the sauce thicken on a medium fire for about 15 minutes.
Finely chop several sprigs of parsley with half a garlic clove and mix with 3 tablespoons of breadcrumbs and one of grated parmesan.
Spread this mixture on each slice of fried eggplant then put a piece of mozzarella at the center and roll each one up, fixing them with a toothpick.
Spread 2 tablespoons of tomato sauce on the bottom of an oven dish, lay the rolls on this and cover them with the remaining sauce and a bit of parmesan. Cook in an oven at 350° F (180° C) for about ten minutes.

If you cannot find...
Mozzarella and parmesan: you can simply leave them out or use another kind, like Swiss cheese.

Mozzarella in carrozza

This Neapolitan appetizer is by now commonly prepared all over Italy. It is easy to make, and even if the ideal ingredient is mozzarella, one could substitute any other soft cheese with a delicate flavor.

Ingredients *(For 4)* :
White sandwich

Bread	*8 slices*
Mozzarella	*4 slices*

2 eggs
Milk, breadcrumbs, seed oil, salt, pepper

Preparation:
Cut off the crusts of bread and moisten the slices in a little cold milk. Make 4 sandwiches with the mozzarella. Press them firmly together, particularly at the edges, then dip them in the egg with salt and pepper. To finish, dip each sandwich in the breadcrumbs, making sure they are well covered, even around the edges. Heat quite a lot of oil in a pan and fry the sandwiches until they are golden on both sides. Put them on oil-absorbing paper for a moment and serve hot.

Olive ascolane

Olive ascolane
(Olives Ascoli-style)

These appetizing tit-bits are a specialty of the Marche region. It is rather long and challenging to make them, but the result is truly worth it. For several years the packaged food industry has had fresh or frozen ready-for-frying Ascoli-style olives on the market, but the quality is not always as good. To make this dish it is indispensable to get giant green olives.

Ingredients *(For 4) :*

40 large green olives

Ground pork	*4 oz (100 g)*
Ground veal	*4 oz (100 g)*
Ground chicken breast	*4 oz (100 g)*

2 eggs

Grated parmesan cheese, breadcrumbs, olive oil, white dry wine, seed oil, celery, carrots, onion, salt, pepper

Preparation:

Finely chop a piece of onion, carrot and celery and brown in 2 tablespoons of olive oil. After a few minutes add the three kinds of finely ground meat. Let the flavors blend for a few minutes, then sprinkle on a little wine and let it evaporate. Cook the meat for 15 minutes then add salt and pepper. The result should be quite dry. Mix in 2 tablespoons of parmesan and an egg yolk. Pit the olives. If you don't have the precise tool for doing this, cut them on a spiral with a sharp knife (making sure not to break them) and remove the olive pit. Stuff each olive with a bit of meat and then dry them on the outside. Beat an egg with the left-over white of the other egg, salt and pepper. Dip the olives in the egg and then in the breadcrumbs so that they are well and thoroughly covered. Heat a good amount of seed oil in a pan and fry the olives on a moderate flame until they are uniformly brown. Place them for a moment on oil-absorbing paper, then serve piping hot.

PARMIGIANA DI MELANZANE
(Eggplant Parma)

Despite being named for Parma which is in Emilia-Romagna, this dish is one of the most celebrated specialties of southern Italian cooking. The name is due to the large amount of parmesan cheese used. Depending on the region, the dish is enriched with other ingredients (mortadella, salami, hard-boiled eggs), but the recipe we offer is the most usual one. If you cannot get either mozzarella or parmesan it would be better to decide against making this dish – it would lose its best qualities!

Ingredients *(For 4) :*
3 large eggplants

Tomato pulp	*1 lb*	*(500 g)*
Mozzarella	*9 oz*	*(250 g)*
Grated parmesan		
cheese	*5 oz*	*(150 g)*

Fresh basil, garlic, oil, salt, pepper

Preparation:
Peel the eggplants and cut them into

Parmigiana di melanzane

quite thin slices. Place them in layers on an inclined cutting board, salting each layer.

Leave them to drain for an hour. Then rinse, dry, and fry them in abundant, extremely hot oil.

Prepare a tomato sauce as indicated in the recipe for *Pasta al pomodoro* in this section, and add 2 tablespoons of oil, a clove of garlic, and a few fresh basil leaves. In an oven dish, alternate layers of eggplant, thin mozzarella slices, and tomato sauce with grated parmesan.

End with a layer of tomato sauce. Put the dish into a 350° F oven (180° C) for about 20 minutes. Served warm or tepid, but also good cold.

PIZZA MARGHERITA

This pizza, the simplest and best known of all, is named for a queen of Italy.
At the beginning of this century a Neapolitan baker dedicated a pizza to her that contained the three colors of the Italian flag (the red of tomato, the white of mozzarella, and the green of fresh basil). Naturally, once you learn the basic recipe for this pizza, you can add vegetables, herbs, or other ingredients to make an infinity of different varieties.

Ingredients *(For 4) :*

Flour	*14 oz*	*(400 g)*
Brewer's yeast	*1 oz*	*(20 g)*
Tomato puree	*14 oz*	*(400 g)*
Mozzarella	*7 oz*	*(200 g)*
Olive oil, fresh basil, salt		

Preparation:

Break the yeast into crumbs and dissolve in 2-3 tablespoons of lukewarm water.

Mix with 2-3 tablespoons of flour and let this dough rise in a warm location

Pizza Margherita

until it doubles in size (about half an hour). Then mix the ball of dough obtained with the remaining flour, 2 tablespoons of oil, a pinch of salt and about half a large glass of lukewarm water. Knead this dough for a long and while energetically until you get a soft, elastic dough which is no longer sticky and does not form cracks. (If it does, add a few more drops of water.) Now form the dough into a ball and cut a cross on the top of it. Place in a lightly floured bowl, cover with a cloth, and let it rise in a warm spot for about 2 hours.

The dough should double in size. Then knead the dough briefly to deflate it and roll it into a fairly thin sheet. Place in a large, oiled baking pan and turn up the edges. Pierce the dough with a fork, brush on some oil and bake in a hot oven (500° F or 250° C) for ten minutes. Then take it out, cover with tomato puree and return it to the oven for another 15 minutes. Next add the mozzarella cut into small cubes, a little oil, and several basil leaves. Bake for another 5 minutes. Serve at once.

PIZZETTE FRITTE
(Small fried pizzas)

A typical Campania dish (where they are called pizzelle) *that makes a tasty appetizer or original snack. If you want to save time, you can use baking powder instead of brewer's yeast.*

Ingredients *(For 4)* :

Flour	*11 oz (300 g)*
Brewer's yeast	*¹/₂ oz (15 g)*
Tomato pulp	*1 lb (500 g)*

Olive oil, fresh basil, garlic, seed oil, salt, pepper

Preparation:

Make a dough as indicated in the recipe for *Pizza Margherita* in this section. While it is rising, prepare a tomato sauce as given in the recipe for *Pasta al pomodoro* (Pasta with Tomato Sauce) See the section "Dried Pasta." Once the dough has risen, knead it briefly to deflate it, and then divide into walnut-sized pieces.

Squash them flat with your hand and then fry them a few at a time in abundant boiling oil. As they become golden, remove and place them on absorbent paper.

Serve piping hot after having put a little tomato sauce on each one.

POLENTA

This humble dish was the main source of nutrition for centuries for farmhands of northern Italy.
Today it is made less often, not only because modern food is much richer and more varied, but also because it requires a bit more time than most dishes.
But polenta is actually ideal to accompany meat cooked in sauce and constitutes a rich and nutritious one-plate meal. The left-over polenta, cut into slices and fried, makes a delicious snack.

Ingredients *(For 4)* :
Polenta   *14 oz (400 g)*
Salt

Preparation:
In a steel pot with a heavy bottom bring to boil about 1¹/₂ quarts (1¹/₂ liters) of water with about ¹/₂ ounce (15 grams) of salt added.
Then sprinkle in the polenta while stirring so that it does not form lumps.

Cook the polenta for about 50 minutes stirring vigorously the whole time with a wooden spoon.

When it is cooked, pour onto a wooden board and serve together with meat stewed in lots of sauce.

Polenta

POMODORI RIPIENI
(Stuffed tomatoes)

There are many Italian recipes for stuffed tomatoes, particularly in the southern and central regions. The majority of these, with some exceptions, use a breadcrumb stuffing and are baked in the oven. Usually the stuffed tomatoes are served tepid or cold and often along with other stuffed vegetables (eggplant, zucchini, bell peppers). The stuffing can be varied by using cooked ham in place of anchovies. One can also add dried mushrooms, minced and cooked, black olives, and capers.

Pomodori ripieni

Ingredients *(For 4) :*
4 ripe, round, firm tomatoes
3 anchovy fillets in oil
Mozzarella	3 oz	(80 g)
Breadcrumbs	3 oz	(80 g)
Grated parmesan	1 oz	(30 g)

Half an onion, parsley, olive oil, salt

Preparation:
Cut the tomatoes in half, carefully remove the inside, eliminating the seeds but keeping the pulp.
Then salt the tomatoes and turn them upside down to drain them of their water for at least half an hour.
Mince the onion with some parsley, the anchovies and the tomato pulp.
Put this mixture in a pan and brown it for several minutes in 6 tablespoons of oil.
Remove from the flame and mix in the breadcrumbs, the parmesan cheese, a little salt and mix well.
Dry the insides of the tomato halves and fill them with small mozzarella cubes and the breadcrumb mixture.
Then put in an oiled baking dish and bake in the oven at 350° F (190° C) for about half an hour.
Serve tepid.

Supplì (Rice croquettes)

This is the Roman version of arancini di riso. In Latium, all take-away pizzas and rosticcerie *sell them, as well as in other regions where they are usually eaten as snacks.*

Ingredients *(For 4) :*

Rice	*11 oz (300 g)*
Tomato pulp	*5 oz (150 g)*
Mozzarella	*4 oz (100 g)*
3 eggs	
Parmesan cheese,	
Breadcrumbs, oil, butter, broth,	
salt, pepper	

Preparation:

With a little oil, butter, and broth prepare a *risotto* as indicated in the recipe in that section. Before adding the broth, however, mix the pureed tomato pulp with the rice and then cook as usual. When the *risotto* is ready, mix in 2-3 tablespoons of grated parmesan. Let it cool, then mix in one egg, pepper, and correct the salt. Form egg-sized oval balls, putting a mozzarella cube in the middle of each one and closing up the *supplì*. Dip in the beaten egg and then in breadcrumbs, covering them well. Fry them a few at a time in deep, very hot seed oil and serve very warm.

Supplì

Torta rustica (Country pie)

Many kinds of savory pies go by this name, but the most popular one is the recipe given here. They are served as main courses, or else as tea-time snacks, on picnics, and for quick lunches.

Ingredients *(For 4) :*

Flour	*1 2/3 cup (250 g)*
Butter	*4 1/2 oz (125 g)*

Ricotta cheese	*7 oz (200 g)*
Cooked ham	*7 oz (200 g)*
2 whole eggs	
Egg yolk, parmesan cheese, nutmeg,	
salt, pepper	

Preparation:

Make a dough with the butter cut in chunks, a pinch of salt, and as much water as needed to obtain a smooth, elastic dough which is firm but not hard. Mince the ham finely and mix with the *ricotta*, the eggs, 4 tablespoons of grated parmesan, salt, pepper and nutmeg.

Divide the dough into two unequal parts.

Roll into a fairly thin sheet and with the larger part, line a buttered cake pan. Pour in the filling and cover it with the remaining dough. Prick holes in the dough with a fork and brush on the beaten egg yolk.

Bake the pie in an oven pre-heated to 380° F (200° C) for about half an hour. Served hot or tepid, it is also good cold.

(Composition created by chef Antonio Sciullo)

SOUPS

Italian regional cooking boasts a long list of soups, though the most characteristic first courses are dried pasta *(pasta asciutta)* specialities to which we have devoted a large section further on. *Pasta asciutta* is the virtually untranslatable term for pasta eaten "dry," i.e. in a sauce rather than in a soup. Nevertheless, an overview of Italian cooking would not be complete without mentioning at least a few of the many soups that appear daily on the family dining table throughout the country, especially in winter.

Minestra di lenticchie

Minestra di lenticchie
(Lentil soup)

Soups based on a mixture of pasta, rice and legumes (beans, chick-peas, peas, lentils) have for centuries substituted for meat courses on the tables of farmers in all parts of Italy. Today they have been re-appraised by modern dietetics as particularly healthy and balanced dishes.

Ingredients *(For 4)* **:**
Dried lentils   7 oz (200 g)

Spaghetti or linguine   *7 oz (200 g)*
Tinned tomato pulp   *5 oz (150 g)*
One onion, garlic, carrot, celery,
  parsley, olive oil, salt and pepper.

Preparation:

Soak the lentils for 8 hours in lots of cold water (so that they are well covered), drain and rinse them and put them into a pot with cold water to cover. Add half the onion, half the carrot and half of the celery stalk, then bring to a boil and cook slowly for at least an hour.

Meanwhile finely chop the remaining onion, carrot, and celery stalk with a clove of garlic and a small bunch of parsley. Brown this mixture in three tablespoons of oil and add the tomato pulp after a few minutes. Add salt and cook for 10 minutes after which add the drained lentils. Let them cook together a few minutes, then add about a pint of slightly salted boiling water and when the ingredients return to a boil, add the pasta broken into lengths of about one inch. Cook for about 8-10 minutes until the pasta is cooked and serve the soup (which should be rather

thick) with a little pepper, a drop of oil and, if you have some, grated parmesan cheese.

If you cannot find...
Dried lentils: substitute dried beans or split peas, but allow them to boil for half an hour longer before adding them to the other ingredients.

Minestrone

This is a soup that utilizes many kinds of vegetables in season and which in north Italy is usually completed with rice while in the South small pasta is used. In the summer it is excellent eaten tepid. In this case the rice or pasta should be cooked al dente *because it will cook through as the soup cools.*

Ingredients *(For 4) :*

Rice	*7 oz (200 g)*
Mixed vegetables	
(already cleaned	
potatoes, carrots	
beans, peas, etc.)	*2 lb (1 kg)*

Pancetta *(bacon)*   *2 oz (50 gs)*
Garlic, onion, parsley, fresh basil,
  olive oil, salt and pepper

Preparation:

Finely chop an onion, a clove of garlic, two basil leaves, and a small bunch of parsley.

Put these into a pot and brown in three tablespoons of oil with the *pancetta* cut into small squares.

Brown on a low flame for about 15 minutes then add the cleaned vegetables cut into small pieces.

Cook this mixture for a few minutes to combine the flavors, then cover with water and bring to a boil in a covered pot.

Add salt, lower the flame and cook for about 40 minutes, after which add the rice, stir, and cook for another 15 minutes or until the rice is done.

Serve, adding pepper to taste and, if you have some, parmesan cheese.

If you cannot find...
Italian *pancetta*: substitute bacon. (However this ingredient is optional. In Italy not everyone uses it).

Pasta e fagioli
(Bean and pasta soup)

There is no region of Italy which does not offer at least one version of this rustic, nourishing soup. Once upon a time lard was used instead of oil, but for modern cooking this is somewhat too heavy.

Ingredients *(For 4)* :

Dried beans	9 oz	(250 g)
Small pasta (ditalini)	7 oz	(200 g)
Prosciutto *with its fat*	3 oz	(80 g)
Tomato sauce	2 tablespoons	

Celery, carrot, onion, bay leaf, grated parmesan, olive oil, salt and pepper

Preparation:

The evening before, soak the beans in plenty of water. The next day drain and rinse them and put them into a pot, covering them with cold water. Add a bay leaf and bring to a boil. Let them cook for about an hour and a half. Salt the water only when they are semi-cooked. Sieve half the beans into a paste, put them back into their broth, and remove the bay leaf.

Pasta e fagioli

Finely chop the *prosciutto* with half an onion, half a carrot and a celery stalk then brown the mixture in three tablespoons of oil. When the vegetables are cooked, add the tomato sauce and a little hot water. When the mixture is reduced, put it into the pot with the beans, adjust the salt to taste and bring once more to a boil. Then add the pasta and cook for another ten minutes. Add a little oil, some pepper and two tablespoons of parmesan to the soup which should be quite thick.

If you cannot find...
Prosciutto: use any kind of bacon or cooked ham.

Ribollita
(Twice-boiled beans)

Ingredients (For 4) :
Dried white beans   *9 oz (250 g)*
Red cabbage   *9 oz (250 g)*
Prosciutto *rind, garlic, onion, celery,*
    tomato paste, oil, salt, pepper

Preparation:
Soak the beans overnight, then boil them with a few pieces of *prosciutto* rind, salting the water only when they are almost cooked. Put half the beans through a sieve or blender and return to the pot. Chop half an onion, carrot, celery, and a garlic clove and sauté with 5-6 tablespoons of oil in a pot (preferably terracotta). When they have dried, add the cabbage cut into strips, a tablespoonful of tomato paste, a little water, salt and pepper. Cook for about 20 minutes, then add the beans with their water. Cook for another 10 minutes.
Let the soup rest for 1-2 days then boil it again and serve with good olive oil, black pepper and, if you like, toasted bread.

Stracciatella

This quickly prepared and nutritious soup originates in Latium, but is also eaten in many other parts of Italy. To enjoy it at its best you should have a good beef broth, but bouillon cubes or the like may also be used.

Ingredients (For 4) :
Beef broth   *approx. 1 qt (1 liter)*
Grated parmesan   *2 1/2 oz   (60 g)*
2 eggs
Salt and pepper

Preparation:
Bring the broth to a slow boil and in the meantime beat the eggs together in a bowl with the parmesan cheese as if for an omelette.
Pour the eggs into the simmering broth and mix rapidly to make the eggs form small lumps. Serve at once with a little pepper.

If you cannot get...
Parmesan: use an aged cheese that is hard enough to be grated and which is no too sharp.

Zuppa di pesce
(Fish soup)

Typical of all the coastal regions, this soup has many variations. The following recipe is the most common one in the South.

Ingredients *(For 4)* :

Mixed fish (polyps, scorpion fish, hake, mullet)	2 ¹/₂- 3 lb	(1¹/₂ kg)
Mussels and clams	2 lb	(1 kg)
Canned tomatoes	13 oz	(400 g)
Bread	4 slices	

Garlic, a hot red chili pepper, parsley, salt, dry white wine, olive oil.

Preparation:

Clean and cut the fish into pieces.
Heat a little oil in a wide pan, cover and cook the mussels and clams on a high flame until the shells open.
Remove the empty shells.
Filter the juice.
Heat 4-5 tablespoons of oil in a pot (preferably terracotta) with 2 garlic cloves and a hot pepper.
Add the polyp cut into pieces, then a little wine, and let it evaporate partially.
Add the tomato and the juice. When the polyps have cooked for 30 minutes, add the fish and continue cooking for 15-20 minutes. Add the seafood, minced parsley, and correct the salt.
Toast the bread and serve with the soup.

Zuppa di pesce

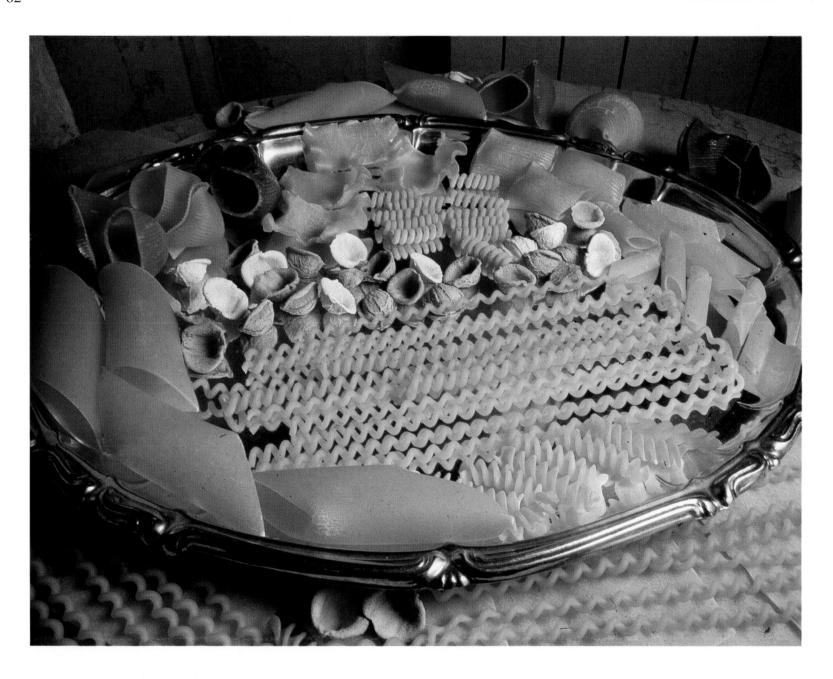

DRIED PASTA

The strong point of Italian cuisine and well loved throughout the country, dried pasta or *pasta asciutta* prods the imagination of cooks (professional or amateur) more than any other dish because it lends itself to countless variations regarding the shape of the pasta and the sauces. Sauces, in fact, can be based on vegetables, fish, meat, cheese, or sausage meats, but also on a few simple ingredients. Among the myriad possibilities, we have had to limit ourselves to the most famous and familiar recipes. They are, on the whole, traditional ones stemming from regional cooking which then became popular throughout the country. However, there are also a few newer recipes which were immediately successful and quickly became part of the repertoire of many restaurants and families. By now pasta has become very well known and a staple abroad as well so that it can easily be found on sale in almost all countries. Before buying, however, it is important to make sure that the pasta is made of hard wheat, since outside Italy you can also find it made of soft wheat. This is an inferior quality which will not remain *al dente*. This means that in the cooking it will turn too soft. Pasta must be eaten when it is still firm in consistency.

To make good pasta there are a few essential rules to follow. First of all the pot must be more than big enough! Use about one quart of water for every ounce of pasta (weighed uncooked). The normal portion for one person is precisely three ounces of uncooked pasta. When the water is boiling add about half an ounce of salt for every quart of water. As soon as the water comes to a boil again, put the pasta in the pot, stir it with a wooden fork, and cook uncovered at a medium heat for the time indicated on the package (usually 7-12 minutes depending on the shape of the pasta). Stir from time to time. When almost done, try the pasta to check its consistency. When it is cooked to your taste quickly drain in a colander. The pasta is then immediately tossed into a hot serving dish and covered with the sauce which should be quickly mixed in before it cools. The final touch is usually a bit of grated cheese that each person adds according to his own taste. In Italy this is almost always parmesan cheese.

Bucatini all'amatriciana
(*Bucatini* Amatrice-style)

*This is a country-style and very tasty
dish that originates in the town of
Amatrice in the region of Latium. The
original recipe calls for guanciale,
quite similar to bacon, which can be
used as a substitute.*

Ingredients (For 4) :

Bucatini	*14 oz (400 g)*
Ripe tomatoes	*14 oz (400 g)*
Pancetta	*3 oz (100 g)*

Onion, olive oil, pecorino *cheese,
hot red chili peppers, salt.*

Preparation:

Boil the water and dip the tomatoes in
it for a few seconds. In this way you
will be able to peel them easily.
Remove their seeds and chop them up.
Put on the pasta water to boil and in
the meantime chop the onion and cut
the *pancetta* into squares. Heat two
tablespoons of oil and brown the onion
and bacon on a very low heat for about
ten minutes, then add the tomatoes and
a little red pepper.

Add salt and cook the sauce on a
medium flame for about 15 minutes
until the liquid evaporates. Correct the
salt.

In the meantime you should have
cooked the *bucatini* according to the
instructions given at the beginning of
this chapter. Drain them while they are
still *al dente* and add the sauce
finishing up with a little grated
pecorino cheese.

If you cannot find...
Fresh tomatoes: substitute canned
ones. In this case too, remove the
seeds.
Pecorino cheese: use an aged, hard,
somewhat sharp cheese.
Pancetta: use bacon.

Bucatini all'amatriciana

Fusilli alla Napoletana
(*Fusilli* Naples-style)

Naples is considered the historic homeland of spaghetti and macaroni, and it is still one of the cities that is most dedicated to the "cult" of pasta. The dish in question possibly owes its name to the fact that it uses the same ingredients as Neapolitan pizza (tomato sauce, mozzarella and anchovies).

It is a happy combination of typically Italian flavors and aromas.

If you want to simplify the preparation of this sauce prepare the tomato sauce according to the recipe for Penne all'arrabbiata *but using only very little red chili pepper.*

Fusilli alla napoletana

Ingredients *(For 4)* :

Fusilli	*14 oz*	*(400 g)*
Canned tomatoes	*14 oz*	*(400 g)*
Mozzarella	*4 oz*	*(100 g)*

4 anchovy fillets in oil

Onion, carrot, celery, garlic, fresh basil, olive oil, salt, pepper or red chili pepper.

Preparation:

Finely chop some onion, celery and carrot together with a clove of garlic. Brown this mixture in four tablespoons of oil and after a few minutes add the tomatoes, a few basil leaves, salt and pepper or red chili pepper. Cook the sauce on a low flame for about twenty minutes then pass it through a sieve so that a thick, homogeneous sauce results. Meanwhile cook the pasta according to the instructions at the beginning of this chapter, drain and pour on the tomato

Maccheroni ai quattro formaggi

Ingredients *(For 4)* :

Macaroni	*14 oz (400 g)*
Melting cheeses	
(such as fontina,	
mozzarella,	
gorgonzola)	*5 oz in all (150 g)*
Parmesan	*3 oz (80 g)*
Liquid cream	*4 oz (100 g)*
Butter, salt, pepper	

Preparation:

Boil water for the macaroni and in the meantime cut all the cheeses except the parmesan into small squares.
Mix them with the cream.
Butter an oven dish that can be used as a serving dish too.
Cook the pasta according to the instructions given at the beginning of this chapter, drain well and put it into a bowl with a large knob of butter, the cheeses and cream, and a tablespoon of grated parmesan. Then put this mixture into the oven dish, cover it with the remaining parmesan and a few thin slices of butter.
Put under the oven grill for a few minutes until it has turned golden on top.

sauce adding strips of mozzarella and anchovies in small pieces. Mix well and serve.

If you cannot find...
Fusilli: substitute any other kind of short or long pasta.

MACCHERONI AI 4 FORMAGGI
(Macaroni with four cheeses)

This dish is served in many restaurants and is often prepared at home to use up odds and ends of cheese. It is not strictly necessary to use Italian cheeses as long as their substitutes have similar characteristics.
Instead of gorgonzola *you can use another rather soft cheese marbled with mold, instead of* fontina *any other semi-hard, tasty cheese will do,* mozzarella *(or at least imitations of it!) can be easily found even abroad, and instead of parmesan, as mentioned, any other hard, tasty cheese that can be grated is acceptable.*

MACCHERONI AL BRANDY
(Macaroni in brandy)

Ingredients *(For 4)* :

Macaroni	*14 oz (400 g)*
Canned tomatoes	*11 oz (300 g)*
Brandy	*¹/₂ glass*
Oil	*¹/₂ glass*
Cream	*2-3 tablespoons*

Parmesan cheese, one onion,
  a clove of garlic, salt, pepper

Preparation:

Finely chop the onion and garlic and brown in oil on a low flame.
Meanwhile put on the water for the pasta. As soon as the onion and garlic have turned color, add the brandy, and immediately after, the chopped tomatoes with their seeds removed.
Let the sauce thicken on a medium flame. At the very end, add the salt, the pepper and the cream.
Mix well.
While the sauce is very hot pour it over the pasta and finish with a generous amount of grated parmesan cheese.

Maccheroni al brandy

Maccheroni
ALLA NORCINA
(Macaroni Norcia-style)

This dish takes its name from the town of Norcia in Umbria which has for centuries specialized in making pork products, sausages in particular.

Ingredients *(For 4)* :
Macaroni
with grooves	*14 oz (400 g)*
Sausages	*7 oz (200 g)*
Cream	*9 oz (250 g)*

One small onion, parsley, dry white wine, grated parmesan cheese, olive oil, salt, pepper

Preparation:
Put on the pasta water to boil and in the meantime chop the onion finely and brown in three tablespoons of oil on a very low flame. After 6-8 minutes add the sausage removed from its skin and cut into small pieces.
Let this turn slightly brown, then add half a glass of wine and let it evaporate over a medium flame. When the sauce is dry add the cream, correct the salt and cook for another few minutes. Turn off the flame and add a spoonful of chopped parsley.
In the meantime you should have cooked the pasta according to the instructions at the beginning of this chapter. When it is *al dente* drain it and immediately add the sausage sauce and some grated cheese.

Pasta alla Norma

This is a famous Sicilian recipe that takes its name from the opera by Bellini, who was born in Catania, as was perhaps this simple but tasty dish.

Ingredients *(For 4)* :
Spaghetti or
other pasta	*14 oz (400 g)*
Ripe cooking	
tomatoes	*1 lb (450 g)*
2 medium size eggplants
| *Hard salted ricotta* | *4 oz (100 g)* |
Garlic, fresh basil, oil, salt

Preparation:
Peel the eggplants and cut them into thin slices on a wooden cutting board. Salt each slice and tilt the board so that the water in the eggplant is allowed to drain for at least half an hour.
Meanwhile heat two tablespoons of oil in a frying pan with a garlic clove and a few fresh basil leaves. Add the tomato (prepared as in the recipe for *Bucatini all'amatriciana*) and cook on a low flame for about 30 minutes, correcting the salt. Then put the sauce through a sieve. Put on the pasta water to boil.
Rinse and dry the eggplant and fry in hot oil.
Make sure the slices do not dry out, then drain the oil and keep them warm. Meanwhile the pasta should have been cooked according to the instructions at the beginning of this chapter.
Add a bit of the grated *ricotta* and the tomato sauce, then the fried eggplant, and the remaining grated cheese.

If you can't find...
Hard, salted *ricotta*: substitute any semi-hard, tasty, slightly sharp cheese.

Pasta alle noci
(Pasta with walnuts)

Walnut sauce is a distinctive tradition of Ligurean cuisine where it is used with pansotti, *triangular ravioli stuffed with herbs and cheese.*
It is prepared in a wooden or marble mortar where the ingredients are crushed with a wooden pestle. But lacking this, or to save time, an electric blender can be used with good results.

Ingredients *(For 4)* :

Pasta   14 oz (400 g)
Shelled walnuts   4 oz (100 g)
Stale bread   1 oz   (25 g)
Milk, olive oil, garlic, salt, white pepper

Preparation:

Put on the pasta water to boil.
Meanwhile soak the bread in a little milk and then squeeze it out.
Grind the nuts in a mortar together with a large garlic clove and the bread.
Add salt and a little pepper, then add 4-5 tablespoons of oil, a little at a time, continuing to grind all the ingredients in the mortar. Once you have obtained a smooth and rather thick paste, mix this with the pasta which you will have cooked according to the instructions at the beginning of this chapter.

You may add some grated cheese, preferably parmesan, if you wish.

Pasta alle noci

Pasta al pomodoro

Pasta al pomodoro
(Pasta with tomato sauce)

To get the best results with this recipe – among the most famous and at the same time simplest of Italian cuisine – you should use fresh ripe plum tomatoes, though you can also get good results with ordinary canned tomatoes. For the pasta to have a truly Italian flavor, however, you must not leave out fresh basil and at the end, a good sprinkling of grated parmesan cheese.

Ingredients *(For 4)* :

Spaghetti or	
other pasta	*14 oz (400 g)*
Fresh or canned	
tomatoes	*1 lb (450 g)*
Parmesan cheese,	
Fresh basil, garlic, olive oil, salt,	
pepper	

Preparation:

Put the water on to boil. Meanwhile heat 3-4 tablespoons of oil in a frying pan together with a garlic clove which you will remove once it is golden brown. Put the peeled, seeded and chopped tomatoes into the frying pan. Thicken the sauce on a rather high flame. Just before turning off the heat add salt, pepper, and a few basil leaves. Meanwhile you will have cooked the pasta *al dente* – that is to say cooked, but still firm in texture – and drained it. Quickly add a handful of grated parmesan. Mix, add the tomato sauce, and mix again.

Penne all'arrabbiata

This famous dish owes its name ("furious" penne) to its distinctly burning hot flavor. It is extremely simple to make, and calls for only a few ingredients easily found everywhere.

Ingredients *(For 4) :*

Pasta in the form of penne	*14 oz (400 g)*
Tomatoes (fresh or canned)	*14 oz (400 g)*
Hot red chili peppers, garlic, olive oil, salt	

Preparation:
Put the pasta water on to boil. Meanwhile heat in a frying pan 4 tablespoons of oil and 2 cloves of garlic. When these turn golden, remove them and add the chopped tomatoes (peeled and seeded, if fresh). Add hot red chili peppers to taste (as much as you can bear!) and cook on a moderate heat for about 15 minutes, correcting the salt in the sauce, which should end up quite thick. Meanwhile you will have cooked and drained the pasta *al dente* according to the instructions at the beginning of this chapter.
Add the sauce and a bit of grated cheese, if you like.

Penne all'arrabbiata

PENNE AL SALMONE
(Penne with salmon)

This dish has no long history behind it, having been invented only in recent years. But it has won widespread popularity so that by now there is hardly a restaurant in Italy that does not have it on the menu.

Ingredients *(For 4)* :

Pasta in the form	
of penne	14 oz (400 g)
Smoked salmon	4 oz (100 g)
Fresh cream	9 oz (250 g)
Brandy or cognac, butter, parsley, salt, pepper	

Preparation:

Cook the pasta according to the instructions at the beginning of this chapter. Meanwhile cut the salmon into strips.

Melt 3 ounces of butter in a large pan, add the salmon and let the flavors blend for a few seconds. Then add a glass of brandy or cognac and let it evaporate. Next add the cream and chopped parsley. Keep it on the flame for another few moments. The sauce should get hot without boiling. Drain the cooked pasta and put it into the pan with the sauce. Mix on a low flame for about a minute, then serve.

PENNETTE ALLA VODKA
(Small penne with vodka)

Of recent invention, this sauce has quickly won great popularity throughout Italy for its very special flavor. It is easy to prepare and the ingredients are so simple that it can be made anywhere.

Ingredients *(For 4)* :

Big or small penne	14 oz (400 g)
Smoked bacon	7 oz (200 g)
Canned tomatoes	14 oz (400 g)
Fresh cream	5 oz (150 g)
Vodka	half a glass
Parmesan cheese	1¹/₂ oz (40 g)
Butter, salt, pepper, oil	

Preparation:

Put the pasta water on to boil and in the meantime heat 2 ounces (50 g) of butter and a tablespoon of oil in a wide pan. Cut the bacon into small squares and brown until golden, then pour on the vodka. Immediately add the tomatoes and let the sauce thicken on a medium flame. Then add the cream and pepper, correct the salt and let the sauce thicken again.

Meanwhile you will have cooked the pasta according to the instructions at the beginning of this chapter. Drain and add the sauce as well as the grated cheese and serve.

If you can't find...
Parmesan: substitute any aged cheese that can be grated.
Olive oil: it is not strictly necessary in this recipe, butter alone will do.

SPAGHETTI AGLIO E OLIO
(Spaghetti with garlic and oil)

For those who want to make a start at cooking pasta, this is a very simple recipe. It is a dish that can be prepared in a few minutes and requires only some of the most ordinary ingredients. For this reason it is the favorite choice on informal occasions when at the last minute you and your friends decide to have a spaghetti party.

Ingredients *(For 4) :*

Spaghetti	*14 oz (400 g)*
Olive oil	*approx. ¹/₂ glass*
Hot red chili peppers, garlic, salt	

Preparation:

Cook the spaghetti according to the instructions given at the beginning of this chapter. Meanwhile heat 2 or 3 cloves of garlic split in half and a piece of hot red chili pepper in a large frying pan. When the garlic turns golden, remove it and the red pepper. Drain the pasta and toss into the frying pan, stir for a few moments on a low flame and serve. You can complete this dish with some fresh minced parsley.

Spaghetti aglio e olio

SPAGHETTI ALLA CARBONARA

This is one of the most beloved pasta dishes in Italy. Originating in Latium, the carbonara *spread throughout the country to become one of the most classic Italian dishes. It is easy to prepare and requires a few ingredients that can be found everywhere. Its name is due to the habit of serving it with plenty of black ground pepper that looks like coal dust.*

Ingredients *(For 4) :*

Spaghetti	*14 oz (400 g)*
Smoked bacon	*5 oz (150 g)*

Parmesan cheese   4 oz (100 g)
3 eggs
Olive oil, salt, black pepper

Preparation:
Put the pasta water on to boil.
Brown the bacon cut into squares in a
small frying pan with 8 tablespoons of
oil until it becomes rather crisp. Beat
the eggs together with the grated
cheese. Cook the pasta *al dente*
according to the instructions at the
beginning of this chapter.
After draining well, return it to its pot,
keeping it on a very low flame, and
mix in the eggs quickly. Stir for a few
moments until the eggs become
creamy. Add the bacon and oil, mix
rapidly and serve after sprinkling with
freshly ground pepper.

If you can't find...
Parmesan cheese: substitute any tasty
aged cheese that can be grated.

Spaghetti alla carbonara

SPAGHETTI ALLA CHECCA

This is a quickly prepared, simple dish that is ideal in summer since it is served cold. Though popular all over Italy it is known by this name mainly in Rome. Unless you can find the precise ingredients called for in this recipe, it is better not to attempt it for the result will be something distinctly different.

Ingredients *(For 4)* :

Spaghetti	14 oz	(400 g)
Fresh tomatoes	1 lb	(450 g)
Mozzarella	5 oz	(150 g)

Fresh basil, olive oil (best if extra-virgin), salt, pepper

Preparation:

Peel and seed the tomatoes, cut them into cubes, salt a little, and place them in a strainer to drain off their water for half an hour. Put the pasta water on to boil.

Mix the tomatoes in a bowl with the mozzarella (which has also been cut into cubes), a chopped garlic clove, about ten chopped basil leaves and 8 tablespoons of oil. Cover the bowl and let the sauce macerate while the pasta cooks. Drain the pasta when it is *al dente* (see the instructions at the beginning of this chapter). Then toss the pasta into the bowl with the sauce, mix quickly, and season with a sprinkling of pepper.

Spaghetti alla checca

Spaghetti alla puttanesca

Originating in Campania and widely found in Latium too, this recipe has a curious name ("Spaghetti in Hooker's Sauce") deriving unquestionably from popular folklore.

Ingredients *(For 4)* :

Spaghetti	*14 oz (400 g)*
Tomatoes, fresh or canned	*14 oz (400 g)*
Tuna in olive oil	*4 oz (100 g)*
Black olives	*4 oz (100 g)*
Capers	*1 oz (25 g)*

Olive oil, garlic, hot red chili peppers, salt

Preparation:

Put the pasta water on to boil while you are browning 1 or 2 garlic cloves and a piece of red chili pepper in 4 tablespoons of oil. Remove the garlic and peppers from the oil as soon as they have turned golden then add the chopped tomatoes, the pitted olives and the capers to the oil. Let the sauce thicken over a medium fire for 10-15 minutes and mix with the pasta which you will have cooked according to the instructions given at the beginning of this chapter.

Spaghetti alle vongole
(Spaghetti with clams)

Two versions of this recipe exist, both widely found and enjoyed along the seacoasts. One is in "red sauce," meaning made with tomatoes to which are added the shelled clams; the other is in "white sauce," meaning without tomatoes, and also differs from the first version in its use of large clams which are served in their shells.

Spaghetti alla puttanesca

Ingredients *(For 4) :*

Spaghetti	*14 oz (400 g)*
Fresh clams	*2 lb (1kg)*
Sieved tomatoes	*7 oz (200 g)*

Garlic, parsley, hot red chili peppers,
  olive oil, salt

Wash the clams and let them soak in a large bowl full of cold salted water for 3-4 hours, changing the water at least once, so that the clams will release the sand inside of them. Then drain the clams and put them in a large pot, adding nothing else. Cover the pot and put it on a high flame for several minutes until the clams have opened. Filter the clam juice left in the pot and keep it for later use. Meanwhile brown 2 garlic cloves until golden in 4 tablespoons of oil, and then discard the garlic. Then add the tomatoes and filtered clam juice. Correct the salt and let the sauce thicken on a high fire. Meanwhile boil the spaghetti as indicated at the beginning of this chapter. Just before you drain the pasta, add the shelled clams and a little minced parsley to the sauce. Mix with the spaghetti and serve hot.

Spaghetti alle vongole

For the version in "white sauce" the procedure is the same, but rather than the tomatoes add about half a glass of white wine to the clam juice. The clams are added to the pasta in their shells.

If you do not find...
Fresh clams: you can use frozen ones that have been thawed at room temperature and added to the sauce just one minute before you take it off the fire. But this way the juice will be more liquid.
Sieved tomatoes: substitute whole ones, fresh or tinned, that have been finely chopped or put through the blender.

SPAGHETTI ALLO SCOGLIO
(Spaghetti reef-style)

Ingredients *(For 4)* :

Spaghetti	*14 oz (400 g)*
Shrimps in their shells	*11 oz (300 g)*
Clams	*18 oz (500 g)*
Squid	*8 oz (200 g)*
Polyps	*8 oz (200 g)*
Tomato puree	*12 oz (350 g)*
Dry white wine	*one glass*
Oil	*¹/₂ glass*
Garlic	*2 cloves*

Parsley (a good-size bunch), hot red chili pepper, salt

Preparation:

Boil the shrimp in slightly salted water for 5 minutes, then shell them and save the cooking water. In a wide pan cook the clams on a high flame until they open, then shell them, leaving only the largest and most decorative ones in their shells. Put their water through a fine sieve and save. In the same pan heat the garlic, red chili pepper and half the chopped parsley in oil, then sauté the squid and polyps in this after cleaning them and cutting them into small pieces. After their flavors have blended, moisten with the wine and let it evaporate on a high flame. Then add a ladle of the clam juice, a ladleful of the shrimp water, and then the tomato puree. Cook the sauce uncovered for about half an hour until it is quite dense and the seafood is cooked. Meanwhile cook the spaghetti. When the time indicated for the sauce is over, remove the garlic and red pepper, add the shelled shrimp and the clams, correct the salt.

As soon as the spaghetti is cooked *al dente* (see the explanation at the beginning of this chapter) drain and toss with the sauce. Let it all blend on a low flame for a few moments, add the remaining chopped parsley and serve.

Spaghetti allo scoglio

Trenette al Pesto

Genoese pesto *is a typical Italian sauce and is the war horse of Ligurian cuisine. It is usually used as a pasta sauce, but it is also good in small quantities to flavor vegetable soups to which it adds a delicious aroma. It was traditionally prepared with a mortar and pestle, and purists still prepare it that way today. The mortar is a marble or wooden recipient in which the wooden pestle is used to crush the ingredients.*
But today it is more common to use a blender which still gives acceptable results. Pesto today is even packaged industrially, but the results are in no way comparable to the results obtained at home with the use of fresh basil.

Ingredients *(For 4)* :

Trenette or spaghetti	*14 oz (400 g)*
Basil	*4 bunches*
Parmesan and	
* pecorino cheese*	*2 oz (50 g)*
Pine nuts	*1 oz (25 g)*
Extra-virgin olive oil, garlic, salt	

Preparation:

Clean the basil with a damp cloth (if you wash it, it will lose a good part of its aroma). Put it into the blender (or mortar if you have one) with the grated cheeses, the pine nuts, 1 or 2 garlic cloves cut into slices and a pinch of salt. Add the oil (about a demi-tasse) a little at a time, blending or crushing it to get a well-blended, homogenized sauce. Meanwhile you should have cooked the pasta in the way indicated at the beginning of this chapter. Drain, add the sauce and serve at once.

Trenette al pesto

Vermicelli alla Siciliana

This recipe is characterized by typical Sicilian ingredients and flavors, is very tasty and easy to make. Besides vermicelli *(which are simply large spaghetti)* one can use any kind of pasta at all, but better if it is the long shape *(spaghetti,* bucatini, *etc.).*

Ingredients *(For 4) :*

Pasta   14 oz (400 g)
Tomatoes fresh
or canned   14 oz (400 g)
Black olives   4 oz (100 g)
Capers   1 oz   (25 g)
Breadcrumbs   4 tablespoons
4 anchovy filets
Olive oil, garlic, hot red peppers, salt

Preparation:

Put the pasta water on to boil and in the meantime brown a garlic clove and a bit of red chili pepper in 3 tablespoons of oil. Remove the garlic and pepper when golden. Add the tomatoes, pitted olives, capers and the anchovies, cut into pieces, to the oil. Add very little salt since the anchovies are already very salty and let the sauce thicken on a medium flame for 10-15 minutes. While the pasta is cooking, brown the breadcrumbs in a smaller frying pan in 4 tablespoons of oil, stirring them frequently (so that they do not burn) until they are nice and golden. When the pasta is cooked and drained, immediately mix in the breadcrumbs and then add the sauce as well.

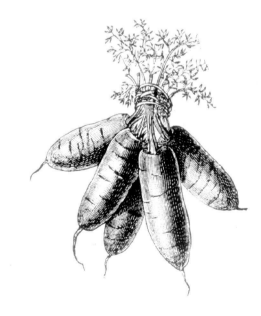

(Composition created by chef Antonio Sciullo)

FRESH PASTA

In Italy the tradition of making fresh pasta, or homemade pasta, is still very much alive despite the fact that times have changed and the number of women grow ever fewer who can dedicate themselves completely to housekeeping and cooking. Homemade pasta is generally made with flour and eggs, but there are some types, typical of southern Italian cooking, which use only flour and water. Then there are the famous *gnocchi* (dumplings) where potatoes are the main ingredient.

Egg pasta can be made in many different shapes, some of which are deliciously stuffed with meat, sausage fillings, cheese, vegetables or fish. In many cases they are very rich and elaborate delicacies, which is the reason they are generally saved for holiday meals. Commercially packaged versions of all the varieties of egg pasta are now widely available in Italy, including the stuffed ones.

However, though some of them are of excellent quality, the more traditional families and many restaurants still stick to homemade pasta. The recipes in this collection are the best known and loved ones, even if they only represent a minimal part of the national repertory in this field. For the sake of practicality, we offer here a basic recipe for preparing egg pasta, while the individual recipes contain instructions on how to cut the various shapes.

Egg pasta
(Basic Recipe)

The traditional quantities call for a medium-sized egg for every four ounces (100 g) of flour, but only practice and experience can guarantee the exact quantities to use because these can vary according to the size of the eggs and the quality of the flour. Keeping these proportions in mind, the quantity of ingredients to use depends on the dish one is preparing. For example, a plate of tagliatelle *requires about one egg and four ounces (100 g) of flour per portion whereas for types to be eaten in soup you will practically halve the quantities (one egg and four ounces of flour for two portions).*

Ingredients *(For 4)* :
Flour   *14 oz (400 g)*
4 eggs
Salt

Preparation:

Use a clean board, preferably wooden, and heap the flour on it. Make a dent in the middle of the heap of flour, sprinkle a little salt and break the eggs into it. Begin to work the eggs into the flour – first with a knife and then, when you have obtained a fairly solid dough, work the mixture by hand energetically and for a long time.

When the dough has become well-blended, firm and elastic, form it into a ball, cover it with a bowl and let it sit for about half an hour.

Clean the board you have been using, if necessary, and roll out the dough with a wooden rolling pin. You must spread the dough into a very thin sheet (1/8 inch or 2-3 millimeters thick) but making sure that it does not have holes. Now the dough is ready to be cut into the desired shape.

Preparation for fresh pasta

CANNELLONI

The true homeland of egg pasta is Emilia Romagna, and there one finds the greatest variety of shapes. Cannelloni *is one of the most elaborate and tasty dishes you can make with egg pasta. It can even be stuffed with a mixture of spinach and* ricotta *(a creamy, fresh cheese) and a little tomato sauce.*

Ingredients *(For 4) :*

Flour	*10 oz (275 g)*
Milk	*1 pt (1/2 liter)*

Ground veal	7 oz	(200 g)
Sausage meat	2 oz	(50 g)
Butter	2 oz	(50 g)
Parmesan cheese	4 oz	(100 g)
2 eggs		
Onion, carrot, celery, oil, salt, nutmeg		

Preparation:

With the eggs and 9 ounces of flour prepare the pasta dough as indicated in the basic recipe for egg pasta and, once you have rolled it into a thin sheet, cut it into many rectangles of about 2 x 3 inches.

Boil the pasta rectangles a few at a time in salted water for a few minutes, then drain and lay them on a clean dishcloth.

Mince a piece of onion, carrot, and celery, and brown them in a knob of butter and oil. After 10 minutes add the ground meat and sausage (skinned and mashed into small bits).

Let it turn brown then add salt, a little grated nutmeg, and cover with a lid. Cook slowly for about half an hour, stirring it often. At the end the mixture should be dry.

Meanwhile prepare the bechamel sauce: melt 2 ounces of butter and mix in the remaining flour without making lumps, then add the hot milk little by little.

Put this mixture on the fire and cook at medium heat, stirring constantly. When the sauce thickens, lower the flame and continue cooking for another 8-10 minutes while stirring. Take off the fire, season with salt and nutmeg, and add 4 tablespoons of bechamel to the meat mixture as well as half the grated parmesan cheese. Spread a little of this stuffing on each pasta rectangle and roll it up into cylinders which you will put into a buttered oven dish.

Cover them with the bechamel sauce, the rest of the parmesan, and a few bits of butter. Put the dish into the oven pre-heated to 180° F (350° C) for about 20 minutes. Serve hot.

Cannelloni

Fettuccine alla Boscaiola
(Woodcutter's *fettuccine*)

This dish is very popular, especially in Latium, where it is usually accompanied by the good wine of the Castelli Romani, the hill country on the outskirts of Rome famous for its wines and for being the popular destination of the Romans' Sunday excursions. Fettuccine *are very much like the Emilian* tagliatelle *but are a little thicker.*

Ingredients *(For 4) :*

Flour	11 oz (300 g)
Fresh mushrooms	9 oz (250 g)
Frozen peas	7 oz (200 g)
Prosciutto *or bacon*	3 oz (80 g)

3 eggs

Dry white wine, half an onion, oil, butter, parsley, salt and pepper

Preparation:

Prepare the pasta with the flour and eggs as indicated in the basic recipe for egg pasta. Roll it into a rather heavy sheet, sprinkle with flour and then roll it up loosely. Cut this roll into strips about a quarter of an inch wide. Let the *fettuccine* dry out on a clean dishcloth for a few hours. Clean and slice the mushrooms. Cook them on a high flame in 3 tablespoons of oil for about 15 minutes with the salt and pepper. At the end, add the minced parsley. Cut up the onion finely and brown in another frying pan with an ounce of butter and 2 tablespoons of oil. Sprinkle on half a glass of wine and when this evaporates add the *prosciutto* or bacon cut into squares and the peas. Add a little hot water,

Fettuccine alla boscaiola

salt and pepper and cook covered for about 20 minutes. Then add the mushrooms to the peas and cook uncovered for 5 minutes. Boil the *fettuccine* in salted water and drain before they become too soft. Add the sauce and grated cheese, preferably parmesan.

GNOCCHI DI PATATE
(Potato dumplings)

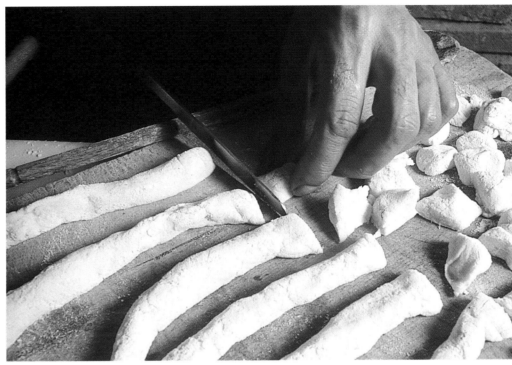
Preparation of gnocchi

Gnocchi *prepared in this way is a Piedmontese dish, but they have long been found everywhere in Italy. They can be eaten with many different sauces, but the most common one is a simple tomato sauce with a good sprinkling of grated cheese. Good alternatives are meat sauce (see the recipe for* Tagliatelle alla bolognese *further on) or a melted cheese, butter and cream sauce (in Piedmont, fontina cheese and melted butter are used).*

Ingredients *(For 4) :*

Floury potatoes	*2 lbs*	*(1 kg)*
Flour	*9 oz*	*(250 g)*

1 egg yolk
Tomato sauce for pasta, salt

Preparation:
Wash the potatoes well and put them unpeeled in a pot. Cover with plenty of cold water and cook for 35-40 minutes after the water has begun to boil. Peel them, and while they are still hot, put them through a potato masher twice.

Mix in the flour, the egg yolk and a little salt. Work this mixture until it is well blended and elastic. Then shape the dough into rolls and cut into pieces of about one inch. Generally they are then rolled over the prongs of a fork to give them their characteristic grooves. Boil the *gnocchi* in simmering salted water and when they rise to the top, drain them carefully and add the tomato

lasagne *long ago became part of the gastronomic heritage in all of Italy. In fact, it is very commonly served in* rosticcerie, *take-away outlets, and cafeterias, though a less rich tomato sauce generally substitutes for the meat sauce.*

Ingredients *(For 4) :*

Flour	*12 oz (360 g)*
Milk	*approx. 1 pt (6 dl)*
Ground beef	*7 oz (200 g)*
Ground pork	*7 oz (200 g)*
Ground sausage	*5 oz (150 g)*
Tomato puree	*4 oz (100 g)*
Butter	*2 oz (60 g)*
Parmesan cheese	*7 oz (200 g)*
3 eggs	
Onion, oil, salt and pepper	

Preparation:

For the meat sauce, chop half an onion and brown it in 2 tablespoons of oil. Add all of the meat, let it brown, then add the tomato puree and thin with a little hot water. Add salt and pepper, cover, and simmer for about 45 minutes.

For the bechamel sauce use the butter,

Gnocchi di patate

sauce or any other sauce, followed by grated cheese (preferably parmesan).

Lasagne alla bolognese

Another great dish from the vast Emilia-Romagna culinary tradition,

2 ounces (60 grams) of flour, the milk, salt and pepper, and proceed according to the recipe for *cannelloni* (see the preceding pages). Then mix this sauce with the meat sauce. For the egg pasta use the remaining 10 ounces (275 g) of flour and the eggs and continue according to the instructions in the basic recipe. After you have rolled out the dough, cut it into rectangles of about 4 x 3 inches (10 x 7 centimeters). Boil the pasta a few rectangles at a time in salted water, then drain and place on a clean dishcloth. Cover the bottom of an oven dish with a little of the sauce and place a rectangle of pasta over it and cover with more sauce and a little grated parmesan. Continue to build up these layers and end with sauce and grated parmesan. Put into an oven pre-heated to 350° F (180° C) for about half an hour.

ORECCHIETTE AI BROCCOLI

Orecchiette *("little ears") is the most traditional type of pasta in Apulia. In this part of Italy they are still mostly homemade and are served with a sauce that is generally not much favored outside of Apulia, made with turnip greens. Here we offer a* version *that may be less traditional in Apulia but is very popular in Rome – a broccoli sauce. We will also teach you how to make the* orecchiette *at home, even if they can be found packaged in shops.*

Ingredients *(For 4)* :
Flour	14 oz (400 g)
Broccoli	2 lb (1 kg)

Lasagne alla bolognese

Orecchiette ai broccoli

Olive oil, garlic, pecorino *cheese, salt, a hot red chili pepper*

Preparation:

Mix the flour with as much water as necessary to make a firm, well-blended and elastic dough. Divide it into little thumb-size rolls and cut these into small pieces about $1/3$ of an inch (1 centimeter). Then crush each piece with your fingers so that it becomes round, flat, and slightly concave at the center. Let the *orecchiette* dry out on a floured board for several hours. Clean the broccoli, cut it into pieces and boil for about 5-6 minutes in salted water. Drain, saving the water to cook the pasta in, if you like. Brown 2 cloves of garlic and a piece of hot red chili pepper in about half a glass of oil. Take out the garlic and chili pepper when they are golden and put the broccoli into the frying pan. Cook it on a low flame until very tender. In the meantime, cook the pasta (not too soft, remember, *al dente*), drain it and add the broccoli with grated *pecorino* cheese.

If you cannot find...
Broccoli: substitute cauliflower, even if the result will be distinctly different from the original version.
Pecorino cheese: substitute another grating cheese that is very tasty and preferably a bit sharp.

Orecchiette verdi con gamberi
(Green *orecchiette* with shrimp)

Ingredients *(For 4) :*

Orecchiette	*12 oz (350 g)*
Shrimp tails	*11 oz (300 g)*
Genovese pesto	*3 tablespoons*
Parmesan cheese, oil, fresh basil, salt	

Preparation:
Make a *pesto* according to the recipe for *Trenette al pesto*.
Meanwhile peel and cook the shrimp in a little oil for 3-4 minutes then salt. A few minutes before draining the *orecchiette*, dilute the *pesto* with 2-3 tablespoons of oil. Add the shrimp and a few hand-torn basil leaves.

Salt the sauce and mix it into the *orecchiette* cooked *al dente* (see the instructions at the beginning of this chapter).

Pappardelle alla lepre
(*Pappardelle* in hare sauce)

Ingredients *(For 4) :*

Flour	*2 heaping cups (300 g)*
Hare meat	*11 oz (300 g)*
Bacon	*7 oz (200 g)*
3 eggs	
Chianti or a similar red wine	*1/2 glass*

Orecchiette verdi con gamberi

Tomato pasté, onion, celery,
carrot, sage, rosemary, parsley,
broth, oil, vinegar, salt, pepper

Preparation:

Make the *pappardelle* as indicated in
the basic recipe for egg pasta, cutting
the dough into strips ⅓ inch wide.
Chop a stalk of celery, a carrot, a small
onion together with a few sage leaves,
a small twig of fresh rosemary and the
bacon. Brown this mixture in a
terracotta pot with 6 tablespoons of oil
on a low flame for a few minutes.
Then add the pieces of hare cut into
small pieces and sauté them over a
high flame until they brown. Add the
wine and let it evaporate, then add a
heaping tablespoon of tomato paste
dissolved in a little hot broth, a
tablespoon of vinegar, salt and pepper,
and cook slowly for about 40 minutes.
Thin the sauce with a little hot broth, if
necessary. At the end, the hare must be
very tender and the sauce dry.
Cook the *pappardelle* and pour on
the sauce. Sprinkle with parmesan
according to taste.

RAVIOLI DI RICOTTA

This is a dish common to many regions
of central and southern Italy. It has
quite a few versions, but they are all
quite similar. In some parts of central
Italy on certain occasions it is
common to sweeten the ricotta with
sugar and then add lemon rind.

Pappardelle alla lepre

Ingredients *(For 4)* :

Flour	*11 oz (300 g)*
Ricotta	*11 oz (300 g)*

5 eggs

Grated parmesan or pecorino *cheese, parsley, cinnamon, nutmeg, butter, salt, pepper*

Preparation:

Prepare the pasta with the flour and 3 eggs (see the basic recipe for egg pasta at the beginning of this section). After rolling out the pasta in a thin sheet, cut it into about 2 x 4 inch (6 x 12 centimeter) rectangles. For the filling, work the *ricotta* with a fork to remove the lumps, then add the remaining eggs, a bit of salt, cinnamon, nutmeg, pepper, a tablespoon of minced parsley, and 2-3 tablespoons of grated *pecorino* or parmesan. Blend well and put a small heap of filling on each rectangle of pasta. Fold each in half and press the edges with your fingers to close them well. Then let them dry for several hours on a clean dishcloth.

Cook the ravioli in salted water that does not boil too fast or they will break open. When cooked but still firm, take them out with a slotted draining spoon and add melted butter or a simple tomato and basil sauce.

If you cannot find...
Ricotta: substitute a soft creamy cheese.

Pecorino: you can use another semi-hard cheese with a marked flavor.

Ravioli di ricotta

Tagliatelle ai Funghi Porcini
(*Tagliatelle* with boletus mushrooms)

Ingredients *(For 4)* :

Fresh tagliatelle	*1 lbs (500 g)*
Fresh boletus	
mushroooms	*9 oz (250 g)*
Brandy	*1 tablespoon*

Parmesan cheese, oil, garlic, salt, pepper

Preparation:

Clean the mushrooms and slice thinly. Heat a garlic clove in 6 tablespoons of oil and remove it when it has turned golden. Sauté the mushrooms in this oil on a medium flame with salt and pepper. Cook them until their water has evaporated, then add the brandy, mix and remove from the fire. In the meantime you should have cooked the *tagliatelle*. Mix in the mushrooms, add the parmesan cheese and serve at once.

Tagliatelle alla Bolognese

This is one of the best-known Italian dishes, at home and abroad. But outside Italy it is often made quite differently. In Italy the egg pasta, cut into long strips, is served with the famous Bolognese meat sauce. We offer here the classic recipe for this sauce. But tagliatelle *can also be served in many other ways. For example, with a simple tomato and fresh basil sauce, or with mushrooms or other vegetables.*

Tagliatelle ai funghi porcini

Ingredients *(For 4) :*

Flour	*11 oz (300 g)*
Ground beef	*5 ¹/₂ oz (150 g)*
Mortadella	
or prosciutto	*3 oz (70 g)*
Chicken livers	*4 oz (100 g)*
Tomato puree	*4 oz (100 g)*

3 eggs

*Dry red wine, onion, celery, carrot,
  butter, oil, salt*

Preparation:

Prepare the egg pasta as indicated in
the basic recipe and roll it out thinly.
Sprinkle with a little flour and roll up
the sheet of dough, but not too tightly.
Take a sharp knife and cut the dough
into strips about ¹/₄ inch (5-6
millimeters) wide. Let these dry out a
little on a clean dishcloth for a few
hours. To make the sauce chop some
onion, carrot, and celery. Brown in one
tablespoon oil and a bit of butter. Add
the ground beef and the *mortadella* or
prosciutto. After a few minutes add a
small glass of good red wine.
When this evaporates add the tomato
puree slightly diluted with water.
Salt and cook covered for about

Tagliatelle alla bolognese

45 minutes, checking now and then to see that the sauce does not dry out too much. Then add the chicken livers cleaned and cut small and cook for another 10-15 minutes.

Boil the *tagliatelle* in salted water for a few minutes (they should remain firm in texture). Quickly drain and cover with the meat sauce and grated parmesan.

If you cannot find...
Mortadella or *prosciutto*: use an equal amount of sausage meat.
Red wine: use white wine or omit the wine entirely.

Tagliolini all'albese
(*Tagliolini* Alban-style)

Tagliolini *is another of the shapes made from egg pasta. Served with the sauce given in this recipe it is a typical Piedmontese specialty. This is a very simple dish, but at the same time most elegant due to the use of white truffles which grow around the town of Alba.*

Ingredients *(For 4) :*

Flour	*11 oz (300 g)*
Butter	*4 oz (100 g)*
Grated parmesan	*4 tablespoons*
3 eggs	
A small white truffle, salt	

Preparation:
Following the basic recipe for egg pasta given at the beginning of this section, prepare the dough and roll it out into a thin sheet. Roll it up loosely and cut it into strips about 1/6 inch (2-3 millimeters) wide. Boil the *tagliolini* in a generous amount of salted water and drain them when cooked but still firm.

Put the *tagliolini* into a warmed bowl and add the butter in thin slices and the grated parmesan. Mix rapidly and grate the truffle over the pasta. Serve quite hot.

Tortelli di magro
(Lean *tortelli*)

This dish is by now widely available commercially. It is native to Emilia-Romagna where homemade tortelli *are served on Christmas Eve.*

Ingredients *(For 4) :*

Flour	*11 oz (300 g)*
Spinach	*1 lb 11 oz (750 g)*
Ricotta	*6 oz (200 g)*
4 eggs	
Grated parmesan, butter, onion, nutmeg, salt, pepper	

Preparation:
Wash the spinach well and cook without water and just a little salt. Squeeze dry, chop finely, and fry in a pan where you have browned a piece of minced onion in butter. Let it cook a few minutes then take off the flame and add the *ricotta*, a small egg, 2-3 tablespoons of parmesan, salt and pepper. The mixture should not be too soft.

Make the egg pasta with the flour and the remaining eggs according to the basic recipe at the beginning of this section, roll it out thinly and cut into 2 1/2 x 5 inch (6 x 12 centimeter) rectangles. Put a little of the filling on each rectangle, fold them in half, and press them closed with your fingers. Cook the *tortelli* in salted water that is not boiling too fast so that they don't break open.

When they are cooked but still firm, take them out with a slotted draining spoon, put them into a soup plate and garnish with melted butter and grated parmesan.

Tortelli di magro

TORTELLI DI ZUCCA
(*Tortelli* filled with yellow squash)

Ingredients *(For 4) :*

Flour	*3 heaping cups*	*(500 g)*
Yellow squash	*4 1/2 lbs*	*(2 kg)*
5 eggs		

Parmesan cheese, nutmeg, butter, sage, salt, pepper

Preparation:

Remove the seeds from the squash and cut it with its rind into slices. Bake in the oven on a buttered pan for 10-15 minutes at 350° F (180° C). When the pulp is soft, remove the rind and put the pulp through a sieve. Dry out the squash puree in a pan with 2 or 3 sage leaves and 2 ounces (50 grams) of melted butter. Stir, add salt and pepper, season with a good amount of grated nutmeg. Then remove from the flame and add a handful of grated parmesan. Make the pasta as follows: heap the flour on a board and make a dent in the center. Break the eggs into the dent and mix, first with a knife and later with your hands. Knead vigorously until you have obtained a homogeneous, elastic, and firm dough. Let this rest for an hour under a dishcloth, then roll out into a thin sheet and cut into rectangles. Place some squash mixture on each of the rectangles, bend them in half and press the edges closed. Boil the *tortelli* a little at a time in slowly boiling salted water. Drain with a slotted spoon and put them into a heated soup tureen. Season each layer with butter, a few sage leaves and grated parmesan.

TORTELLINI IN BRODO
(*Tortellini* in broth)

Tortellini in brodo

This is also an Emilia-Romagna specialty where the pasta changes name from one area to another: cappelletti, agnolini, *etc. Although in other parts of Italy the* tortellini *are generally eaten "dry" (with meat sauce or tomato sauce, or simply with butter), in their native region they are usually served in a good beef and chicken broth. Making them is rather a long and challenging process, but the* result is far superior to the commercial packaged ones.*

Ingredients *(For 4)* :

Flour	7 oz	(200 g)
Beef	5 oz	(150 g)
Prosciutto	2 oz	(50 g)
Chicken meat	2 oz	(50 g)
Good meat broth	3 pts	(1 ½ liters)
2 whole eggs		

One egg yolk, parmesan cheese, onion, butter, nutmeg, oil, salt

Preparation:

Grind the beef, chicken, and ham together. Mince some onion and brown it in a tablespoon of oil with a little butter.

Next add the meat mixture and cook covered on a low flame for

30-40 minutes with a pinch of salt. When cooked, the meat should be quite dry. Flavor with a little nutmeg, then add the egg yolk and a few spoonfuls of grated parmesan. Let this mixture rest for a few hours in a cool place so that it becomes more compact.

With 2 eggs and the flour, prepare the pasta dough as indicated in the basic recipe at the beginning of this section. Cut it into one-inch squares (3 centimeters).

Put a ball of the meat filling onto each square and fold the pasta into a triangular shape, pressing the edges closed with your fingers. Lay out the *tortellini* on a clean dishcloth and let them dry for several hours, then place them carefully in the slowly simmering broth where they will cook in a few minutes. Serve in the broth with a little grated parmesan.

If you cannot find...
Prosciutto: use an equal amount of ground sausage.

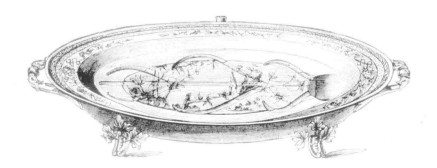

Risotto ai gamberi

RICE

Although Italy certainly does not have the exclusive on rice, this grain has an important place in the country's cuisine, especially in the North. Moreover, Italy is one of the major rice producers of the world and the quality of its rice is exceptionally high. Italians cook rice in many variations, many of which are similar to the preparations in other countries. But there is one way which is typically Italian: *risotto*.

It seems that this way of cooking rice was invented in Lombardy, a region that along with Veneto and Piedmont boasts some of the oldest Italian rice recipes. In this section we have collected some of the most popular of those recipes. In recent years, new and successful preparations considered variations of the basic *risotto* recipe have become more and more popular. Examples are the cream of shrimp *risotto*, champagne *risotto*, or "garden" *risotti*. Once you have

learned the basic procedure, you can make a great variety of *risotto* by simply changing the seasoning or the other ingredients (vegetables, fish, sausage meats, cheeses, etc.).

Risotto
(Basic Recipe)

This procedure is simple and always produces good results as long as you keep a few tips in mind.
Above all the broth or water that you add to the rice must always be boiling hot. In addition it should be added a little at a time, especially towards the end of the cooking, so that you do not get a liquid risotto.
The main characteristic of this dish is that it is soft and creamy, but not watery. The type of rice best suited for this kind of preparation is the slightly round and firm kind.

Ingredients *(For 4) :*
Rice   14 oz (400 g)
Broth (preferably
* of meat)   approx. 1 qt (1 liter)*
Parmesan cheese (or similar), butter,
* one small onion, dry white wine, salt,*
pepper

Preparation:

Mince the onion and brown it in 2 ounces (50 grams) of butter on a very low flame.

Be careful it doesn't burn. When soft, add the rice and stir for a couple of minutes until all the butter has been absorbed and the rice is shiny.

Sprinkle with half a glass of wine (this is not essential and some cooks omit it) and let it evaporate. Then begin adding the boiling broth, one ladleful at a time.

Stir frequently and each time the broth has been absorbed, add more.

After about 15 minutes the rice should be done.

If the rice seems too hard to you, cook it a little longer, but keep in mind that it should be slightly *al dente* - that is, not mushy.

Correct the salt, add pepper if you like, and as soon as you turn off the flame, mix in a knob of butter and 2-3 tablespoons of grated parmesan. Let it rest for a minute then serve.

The rice should be dry but slightly creamy.

Risotto ai Funghi
(Mushroom *risotto*)

This dish is found all over the country, particularly in the mountain regions where the prized boletus mushrooms grow. This dish is best made with fresh pores when in season and otherwise, dried mushrooms.

Ingredients *(For 4)* :

Rice	14 oz (400 g)
Fresh mushrooms	14 oz (400 g)

Dry white wine, broth, half an onion, garlic, parsley, grated cheese, oil, butter, salt, pepper

Risotto ai funghi

Preparation:

Clean the mushrooms removing the bottom of the stem. If you use wild mushrooms do not spoil the flavor by washing them, but rub delicately with a damp sponge and then cut them into slices or pieces.

Brown a clove of garlic in 2 tablespoons of oil, removing it when it is golden.

Add the mushrooms, salt and pepper, and cook for 10 minutes. Add some minced parsley.

Brown the minced onion in a pot with 3 ounces of butter, then add the rice and cook according to the basic recipe given in the beginning of this section. When the rice is half cooked add the mushrooms.

Before serving add a knob of butter and a handful of grated cheese.

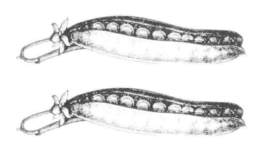

Risotto ai gamberi
(Shrimp *risotto*)

Ingredients *(For 4)* :

Rice	*12 oz (350 g)*
Whole shrimps	*1 1/3 lb (600 g)*

Cognac, dry white wine, onion,
 garlic, celery, parsley,
 tomato paste, fresh cream, oil, butter,
salt, whole peppercorns

Preparation:

Boil ³/₄ quarts of water with a glass of wine, some celery and onion, a garlic clove, parsley and some peppercorns. When the water boils, salt and add the shrimp heads and shells, setting the tails aside.

Risotto ai gamberi

Let this simmer for about 20 minutes, then add the shrimp tails, boil one more minute and drain. Put the shrimp soup through a sieve. Sauté half an onion in 1 ounce (30 grams) of butter and a tablespoon of oil, add the rice and after a minute sprinkle on a little cognac. Let it cook adding the shrimp soup a little at a time as it is absorbed. About 5-6 minutes before the rice is done, add the shrimp tails, a tablespoon of tomato paste and 2 tablespoons of cream.
Before serving, sprinkle with some chopped parsley and decorate with a few whole shrimp.

Risotto alla Milanese
(*Risotto* Milanese-style)

This risotto, *which has the color and aroma of saffron, is one of the true classics of the Lombard kitchen. There is hot debate over the question of whether or not to add wine to the rice after it has been fried. Although many like the wine, it seems that it was not included in the original recipe. So you can suit yourself after having tried it both ways. Risotto alla milanese is also often turned into a one-plate meal by serving it with roast quail or Ossibuchi alla milanese (see the section Meat and Poultry).*

Ingredients *(For 4) :*

Rice	14 oz	(400 g)
Beef marrow	2 oz	(50 g)
Butter	3 oz	(80 g)

Meat broth, a medium-sized onion, a packet of saffron, parmesan cheese, salt

Preparation:
Briefly scald the beef marrow in boiling water, remove the red membrane and mince. Mince the onion too and and put it into a frying pan where you have heated the marrow with 2 ounces (30 grams) of butter. Brown slowly for at least ten minutes, paying attention that the onion neither burns nor takes on too much color. Then add the rice and proceed according to the basic recipe. Dissolve the saffron in the last ladleful of broth you use. Just before removing from the fire add the remaining butter in small pieces and a handful of grated parmesan.

If you cannot find...
Beef marrow: you can slightly increase the amount of butter used in the browning.
Parmesan: use any tasty, hard, grating cheese.
Saffron: without this ingredient you can make all kinds of other *risotti*, but not the Milanese.

Risotto alla Pescatora
(Fisherman's *risotto*)

This dish is found all over the country in many variations according to the fish used. What is almost never missing are shellfish and squid however. For the rest, you can add what you like and perhaps use the ingredients in different proportions. White wine is optional.

Ingredients *(For 4) :*
Rice   14 oz (400 g)

Tomato (canned)	*7 oz (200 g)*
Fresh mussels	
* and clams*	*1 lb (500 g)*
Whole shrimp	*7 oz (200 g)*
Small squid	*5 oz (150 g)*
Garlic, parsley, onion,	
* oil, salt, pepper*	

Preparation:

Clean the mussels and clams and soak them in salted water for several hours, then drain and put them into a pan. Put them on a high flame until they open, then shell and save the water they contained for later use. Parboil the shrimp in salted boiling water and shell them. Save the water.

Clean the squid and cut them up in small pieces.

Heat 2 tablespoons of oil in a pan and brown 2 whole cloves of garlic, removing them when they have turned golden. Add the tomato, salt, pepper, and after a few minutes, the squid. Cook for 7-8 minutes then add the shrimp and seafood.

Cook another 2 minutes. Brown half a minced onion and a small bunch of parsley in a pot.

Add the rice, let it fry for a few minutes, and then sprinkle with the water from the seafood.

When this has been absorbed, add more salted boiling water (fish broth would be ideal) as needed to cook the rice (see the basic recipe at the beginning of this section).

About 2 minutes before the rice is completely cooked, add the tomato sauce and the seafood.

Correct the salt if necessary and add pepper.

If you cannot find...
Fresh seafood: use frozen ingredients.

RISOTTO ALLE ORTICHE
(*Risotto* with nettles)

Ingredients *(For 4) :*

Rice	*12 oz (350 g)*
Fresh nettle greens	*14 oz (400 g)*
Cream	*4 oz (100 g)*
Swiss cheese	*2 oz (50 g)*
One small onion, dry white wine,	
* broth, butter, oil, parmesan*	
* cheese, salt*	

Preparation:

Chop the onion finely and brown in 1 ½ ounces (40 grams) of butter and a tablespoon of oil. Meanwhile wash the nettles and cook them in the water remaining on the leaves with a little salt. When they are tender put them through the blender. Add the rice to

Risotto alle ortiche

the onion and let the flavors blend while stirring constantly. Then add a little wine and let it evaporate. Mix in the nettles, stir well, and begin to add the hot broth one ladle at time as it is absorbed. About 5 minutes before it is cooked, add the cream and the cheese cut into small pieces.

Before serving, add pepper and 2-3 tablespoons of parmesan after correcting the salt.

Risotto al vino
(*Risotto* with wine)

Ingredients *(For 4)* :

Rice	*12 oz (350 g)*
Barbera or a similar red wine	*1 ¹/₂ glasses*

Meat broth, butter, parmesan cheese, lard, an onion, salt, pepper

Preparation:

Chop the onion and a piece of lard together and brown in a pan with a small knob of butter.

After about 10 minutes add the rice,

let the flavors blend well then moisten with the wine which you have warmed a little. When the wine has been absorbed, begin to add the broth a

little at a time. Before serving add another bit of butter and a handful of grated parmesan. Let it rest for a few minutes and serve.

Risotto al vino

Sartù di riso
(Rice sartù)

This is a sumptuous Neapolitan dish derived from the aristocratic cuisine of past centuries. Still today it is served on special festive occasions like Christmas.

Ingredients *(For 4) :*

Rice	*11 oz (300 g)*
Canned peas	*5 oz (150 g)*
Chicken livers	*7 oz (200 g)*
Sausage	*4 oz (100 g)*
Canned tomatoes	*4 oz (100 g)*
Mozzarella	*5 oz (150 g)*
4 eggs	

Onion, broth, breadcrumbs, parmesan cheese, oil, butter, salt, pepper

Preparation:

Prepare a normal *risotto* (see the basic recipe) and let it cool off to tepid. Then add 2 raw eggs and 3-4 tablespoons of grated parmesan cheese.

Mince a piece of onion and brown it in a knob of butter with 2 tablespoons of oil. After a few minutes add the skinned sausage cut into small pieces, the chicken livers cleaned and cut up small, and the peas.

Let the flavors mix then add the tomato pureed in a blender, 2 tablespoons of broth, and let the sauce thicken on a low flame. Add salt and pepper.

Hard boil and shell 2 eggs. Grease an oven mold with butter and cover with breadcrumbs. Then line the sides and bottom with about three - fourths of the rice.

Fill the center with the livers, sausage, hard boiled eggs and sliced mozzarella. Cover with the remaining rice and press down lightly on the mixture.

Put in an oven pre-heated to 350° F (180° C) for half an hour, then wait about ten minutes before removing the *sartù* from the mold onto a plate.

If you cannot find...

Parmesan or mozzarella: substitute the first with a hard, tasty cheese that can be grated, and the second with a fresh rather bland cheese that will melt in the oven.

Maialino al latte

MEAT AND POULTRY

Meat figures in many traditional Italian recipes, and not only pork and lamb, which until a few decades ago were the most commonly found on Italian tables. In fact, mainly in north Italy, a great number of recipes include beef. Among these there are not only tasty country-style dishes, but some true culinary masterpieces, thanks in part to the excellent quality of the ingredients. One need only remember, for example, *Brasato al Barolo* (Braised beef in Barolo) which, due to the use of the superb Piedmontese wine, is one of the greatest dishes of Italian regional cooking.

With meat, as with other kinds of food, proverbial Italian imagination and creativity have often made up for the scarcity of the most choice foods and have known how to transform a few simple ingredients into extremely delicious dishes. Thus even the most economical cuts of meat, such as offal and nervy parts, which had often been considered little more than refuse, became the main ingredients of distinctly appetizing and flavorful specialties. Family cooking in Italy, particularly in Latium, is especially rich in dishes of this kind. Today these preparations are no longer considered common but, on the contrary, have acquired the fascination and the mark of the most traditional and genuine cooking.

ABBACCHIO ALLA ROMANA
(Lamb Roman-style)

In Rome, as everywhere in Latium, lamb is very popular. Suckling lamb (agnello), *considered best, is called* abbacchio *in Latium and can be recognized by its light pink color which is particularly delicate and tender.*

There are many Roman recipes for lamb, but the most typical is Costolette a scottadito *("burned-finger" lamb chops), where the chops are simply roasted on a brazier and seasoned with salt and pepper.*

The name comes from the custom of picking the chops up by the bone with your fingers.

The recipe given here is more elaborate, but it is one of the most typical and tasty to be found in central Italian cooking.

It is advisable to get very young lamb for this.

Abbacchio alla romana

Ingredients *(For 4)* :
Lamb cut into
  pieces   approx.   2 ¹/₂ lb (1.2 kg)
3 salted anchovies
Dry white wine, white wine vinegar,
  garlic, rosemary, sage,
  olive oil, salt, pepper

Preparation:
Remove any excess fat from the meat
and put the pieces into an oven dish.
Season with some sliced garlic, sage

leaves, and rosemary. Add
4-5 tablespoons of olive oil, salt and
pepper, and cook in the oven at 390° F
(200° C) for about 45 minutes.
Turn the meat from time to time and
baste it with wine (about half a glass
in all).
Meanwhile rinse the anchovies and
remove the backbone and fins.
Then crush the anchovies with a clove
of garlic and a sprig of rosemary.
Dilute this mixture with 2-3
tablespoons of vinegar so as to obtain
a sauce.
Brush it on the already well-browned
lamb and return to the oven for a few
minutes.

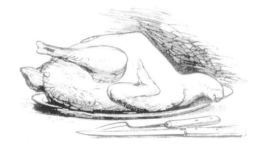

AGNELLO IN FRICASSEA
(Fricassee of lamb)

*This lamb recipe is found in central
Italy, especially Latium. It is a
traditional Easter dish and is known
by different names with ingredients
that vary somewhat. In Liguria, for
example, a version of this dish is
prepared which calls for artichoke
wedges. In other places boiled
potatoes are added to the meat and
allowed to take on the flavor of the
gravy for a while before it finishes
cooking.*

Ingredients *(For 4)* :
*Lamb breast and
  shoulder   approx. 2 ¹/₂ lb (1.2 kg)
3 eggs
One lemon, dry white wine,
  garlic, parsley, broth, oil,
  butter, salt, pepper*

Preparation:
In a wide, low pan, best if made of
terracotta, crush and brown a garlic
clove in 2 ounces of butter and a
tablespoon of oil.

Then brown the lamb in it cut into equal-size pieces. As soon as it takes on a little color, add a small glass of wine. Let it evaporate. Then add a ladleful of hot broth, salt, pepper, and cover. Cook on a low flame for about an hour. Beat the eggs with the lemon juice, salt and pepper and a tablespoonful of chopped parsley. When the meat is tender, remove from the fire and add the egg mixture while mixing to obtain a creamy sauce. Serve at once.

ARISTA

This is a very old dish from Florence which is hard to find outside Tuscany, but which is worth trying to make if you can find the suitable meat. Its name comes from the Greek ariston meaning "excellent." Tradition says some Greek prelates to the Council of 1430 in Florence uttered that word when tasting this dish.

Ingredients *(For 4)* :
Boned
  pork loin   *approx.* 2 ¹/₂ *lbs* *(1.2 kg)*

Agnello in fricassea

*Garlic, rosemary, olive oil, salt,
  pepper*

Preparation:

Finely chop two garlic cloves with a sprig of fresh rosemary and salt and pepper. With a thin sharp knife cut some quite deep openings in the meat and push the aromatic mixture into

them. Put the meat into an oven dish with two tablespoons of oil and roast first at a high temperature, 445° F (230° C) until browned, then lower to 350° F (180° C) for about an hour and a half. Salt and pepper the meat while roasting, turning and basting it frequently with its juices.If it does not produce enough liquid, add a few tablespoons of dry white wine or broth.

Arista

Bistecche alla pizzaiola
("Pizza" steak)

This dish is originally from Campania, but now it is found almost everywhere. It is very quick and easy to prepare. The name comes from the ingredients added to the meat and which are indispensable in the preparation of a pizza sauce: tomato and oregano. Some people also add at the last minute another pizza ingredient – a few slices of mozzarella which are allowed to melt a little with the warmth of the meat. This is not part of the original recipe, but it makes for a richer, more nutritious dish.

Ingredients *(For 4) :*

*Sliced lean
Beef   approx. 1 lb. (500 g)
Tomato puree   9 oz (250 g)
Olive oil, garlic, oregano, salt,
  pepper*

Preparation:

If the slices of beef are very wide, cut them a little smaller and as near equal size as possible. Use a large

Bistecca alla pizzaiola

Braciole al vino
(Pork chops in wine)

In the version we give here, this is a typically Tuscan dish. In other parts of Italy white wine is used rather than red, and sometimes different aromatic herbs from the ones in the Tuscan recipe. Sage and rosemary, in particular, are often added. In all cases we are dealing with a tasty, country-style dish where the wine also serves to consume the fat and thus lighten the taste.

Ingredients *(For 4)* :
4 pork chops (with bone)
Red wine (Chianti is best)
Olive oil, parsley, garlic, salt, pepper

Preparation:
A few hours before cooking, marinate the meat in 2 tablespoons of oil, a garlic clove, half a glass of wine, a little parsley, and a pinch of pepper. Cover and keep in a cool place. Before cooking, drain and dry the pork chops, then brown them in a frying pan with 2 tablespoons of oil on a

frying pan or even two, since the slices of meat should not overlap.
Heat a crushed garlic clove in 2-3 tablespoons of oil. Place the meat in the pan and cook on a high flame until it browns (about a minute on each side) then remove and keep warm. Put the tomato puree into the pan and thicken on a high flame, then put the meat back in.

Add salt and pepper and turn in the sauce on a medium flame for several minutes.
Season with a good pinch of oregano and serve at once.

If you cannot find...
Tomato puree: use normal tinned tomatoes put through the blender and sieved to remove the seeds.

Braciola al vino

medium flame. When they have turned golden on both sides sprinkle them with very finely chopped parsley and garlic and add a glass of wine. Turn down the heat and cook for about 20 minutes. When ready, the sauce should be quite thick (if necessary add a little hot water during the cooking).

If you cannot find...
Chianti: you can use another full-bodied, dry red wine rather than this typical Tuscan red.

Brasato al Barolo
(Braised beef in Barolo wine)

Ingredients (For 4) :
Beef roast   *approx. 2 lbs*   *(1 kg)*
Barolo wine   *1 bottle*
An onion, a carrot,
* a stalk of celery, garlic,*
* bay leaf, sage, rosemary, cloves,*
* cinnamon, oil, butter, salt, pepper*

Preparation:
The evening before, marinate the roast in the wine and the vegetables cut into

pieces. Cover and keep in a cool place. The next day drain the beef and brown in a pot with 2 tablespoons of butter and a tablespoon of oil. When it has browned, add a mixture of chopped rosemary, 2 or 3 sage leaves, and a clove of garlic. After a few minutes also add the vegetables used to marinate the beef plus a bay leaf, two cloves, and a pinch of cinnamon. Let the flavors blend for a few minutes, add salt and pepper and a little of the wine from the marinade. Cook covered on a very low flame for about 2 1/2 hours, adding all the wine a little at a time.

After cooking, the meat should be very tender and the gravy quite thick. (If the wine should not provide enough liquid, add a little hot water.) When done, sieve the gravy and serve over the sliced beef.

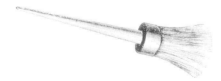

Brasato al Barolo

CODA ALLA VACCINARA
(Braised ox tail)

This is an ancient recipe from the Roman pauper's kitchen and today is usually only found in families and restaurants which stick to the old traditions. However, it is such a savory dish that it deserves to be remembered. Don't be too astonished by the use of chocolate – it is an old stroke of genius that gives the gravy the right taste and a special consistency, but which does not betray its presence in the general harmony of the various flavors.

Ingredients *(For 4) :*

One ox tail	4 ¹/₂ lbs	(2 kg)
Tomato puree	2 lbs	(1 kg)
Green celery	3 bunches	
Bitter-sweet chocolate	1 oz	(20 g)

A large onion, dry white wine, oil, salt, pepper

Preparation:

Have the butcher cut the ox tail into pieces.
Boil a large pot of water and parboil

Coda alla vaccinara

the ox tail for about 10-15 minutes on a low flame to remove excess fat. Then drain the ox tail and brown it in a pan with half a glass of warm oil.
When both sides have browned, add the onion chopped together with a stalk of celery and let the flavors blend for a few minutes. Then moisten with a small glass of wine and let it evaporate. Then add the tomato, salt, pepper, and the rest of the celery cut in pieces removing the strings.
Cook on a low flame for about 2 ½ hours. Towards the end of this cooking time, add a little hot water if necessary. About 20 minutes before it is done, add the pieces of chocolate to the gravy.

If you cannot find...
Tomato puree: use ordinary tomato pulp (a little more than the amount of puree indicated) put through the blender and sieved.

Coniglio [o pollo] alla cacciatora
(Rabbit [or chicken] hunter's style)

Unlike some countries, in Italy rabbit meat is very popular. Today, because people are better off and have less time to devote to dishes requiring long cooking, rabbit meat is not used as much as other meats considered more choice or at least more quickly prepared. Nevertheless some recipes for rabbit are still among the most typical of the Italian culinary tradition. The basic rabbit recipes are all perfectly suitable for the use of chicken. The one that follows, in particular, is made with either of these meats in exactly the same way.
Many parts of Italy, particularly the northern and central regions follow this recipe.

Ingredients *(For 4)* :

One cleaned rabbit	approx. 2 lbs	(1.2 kg)
Ripe cooking tomatoes	14 oz	(400 g)
Bacon	3 oz	(80 g)
Butter	2 oz	(50 g)
Dry white wine, flour, an onion, a carrot, a celery stalk, garlic, vinegar, oil, salt, pepper		

Preparation:
Cut the rabbit into medium-sized pieces and rinse in water with some vinegar added.
Dry the pieces and brown them in a pan with butter, a tablespoon of oil, the bacon cut into cubes, a sliced onion and a crushed garlic clove.
When the meat has browned, sprinkle on a tablespoon of flour, stir, and moisten with a glass of wine.
Let this evaporate.
Add the chopped vegetables and the tomato, salt, pepper, and cook for about an hour on a low flame.
When ready the gravy should be quite thick.

Coniglio alle olive

CONIGLIO ALLE OLIVE
(Rabbit with olives)

This is a very popular way of cooking rabbit, particularly in Liguria, although with some variations it is found in Calabria and Sicily. In these two latter regions it is common to add tomato, to use green rather than black olives, and to substitute thyme with other herbs or hot red chili pepper. Like all the other rabbit recipes, this too is perfectly suitable for chicken.

Ingredients *(For 4) :*
One cleaned rabbit   2 lb (1.2 kg)
Olive oil, dry white wine, vinegar,
  broth, thyme, salt, pepper

Preparation:
Cut the rabbit into not too large pieces and rinse them in water and vinegar. Heat 4-5 tablespoons of oil in a pan and brown 2 garlic cloves and the rabbit. When golden, moisten with half a glass of wine. Let this evaporate then add salt, pepper and the olives (with the pits removed), a little hot broth and cook covered on a low flame

for about an hour. If necessary add more broth during the cooking, keeping in mind that the final result should be fairly dry. Just before serving, season with a pinch of fresh or dried thyme.

COSTOLETTE ALLA MILANESE
(Milanese veal chops)

This is one of the oldest and most typically Italian recipes. In fact, the expression alla milanese *is used to mean any food that is breaded and fried. The dish is very similar to the Austrian* wiener schnitzel. *For, in the nineteenth century northern Italy was part of the Austro-Hungarian empire with the ensuing cultural and culinary influences.*

Ingredients *(For 4) :*
4 veal chops
2 eggs
Butter   *4 oz (100 g)*
Breadcrumbs, lemon,
* salt, pepper*

Costolette alla milanese

Preparation:

Flatten the chops lightly with a mallet then dip them in the beaten egg which has been mixed with salt and pepper. Then roll them in the breadcrumbs making sure they are very well covered. Heat the butter in a large frying pan, then fry the chops on a medium flame until golden on both sides. Place them for a moment on paper to absorb the excess oil and serve very hot with a few wedges of lemon.

Cotolette alla BOLOGNESE
(Bolognese veal cutlets)

Although not an exclusively Italian invention, these cutlets (slices of veal, breaded and fried) in certain regions become distinctly Italian because of the ingredients with which they are combined.
The Bolognese recipe is particularly appreciated and popular throughout the country.

Ingredients *(For 4)* :

Veal cutlets	*14 oz (400 g)*
Sliced cured	
prosciutto	*4 oz (100 g)*
Parmesan	
(not very aged)	*2 oz (50 g)*
2 eggs	

Breadcrumbs, flour, butter, oil, salt, pepper

Preparation:

Flatten the cutlets a little, eliminating any fat. Roll them first in flour, then in the beaten eggs mixed with salt and pepper, and lastly, in the breadcrumbs. Fry on a medium flame in a pan containing 2 ounces of hot butter and 2 tablespoons of oil until they are golden on both sides. Then lay them on absorbant paper for a moment and put them in an oven dish. Cover each cutlet with a slice of ham and a thin slice of cheese. Put the cutlets in an oven pre-heated to 300°F (200° C) for a few minutes, just long enough for the cheese to melt.

If you cannot find...
Cured *prosciutto* and parmesan: it is possible to use cooked ham and a cheese such as emmenthal, but in this case the result will be an excellent international recipe and not a Bolognese speciality.

Fagioli con le cotiche
(Beans with pork rind)

This is an extremely rustic, robust, tasty dish. The version given here is Roman style, but not very different from an analogous Venetian dish. Cotica is Roman dialect for pork rind. In Rome the rind of prosciutto is generally used, which is the part of the ham the butcher cuts off in order to slice it. Thus in this case we are again dealing distinctly with a dish of humble origins.

Ingredients *(For 4)* :

Fresh pork rind	*14 oz (400 g)*
Dried beans	*11 oz (300 g)*
Canned tomatoes	*9 oz (250 g)*
Cured prosciutto	
in one slice	*3 oz (80 g)*

Garlic, onion, parsley, salt, pepper

FEGATO ALLA VENEZIANA
(Venetian-style liver)

This is one of the most typical Venetian dishes, but is well-known throughout the country.

Ingredients *(For 4) :*

Sliced calf's
liver   approx. 1 lb (500 g)
White onions   approx. 1 lb (500 g)
Milk, olive oil, salt, pepper

Preparation:

Cover the thinly sliced liver with milk and let it rest in a cool place for 1-2 hours.

Slice the onion very thinly, place in a large frying pan, and cook covered on a very low flame in 5-6 tablespoons of oil, salt and pepper, for about 40 minutes, adding a little water from time to time to keep it from burning.

Remove the lid and allow the onions to brown a little after which drain, dry, and add the liver.

Cook for 4-5 minutes turning the liver

Fagioli con le cotiche

Preparation:

The evening before, put the beans to soak in tepid water. The next day put them in a pot, cover with cold water, then cook. Scrape the pork rind well and boil for 15 minutes. Drain and cut into strips. When the beans have been boiling for half an hour, add the pork rind and continue cooking for another hour, after which add the salt. Mince the *prosciutto* together with the garlic, onion and parsley and brown in a terracotta pot for a few minutes before adding the tomatoes. Pour in the drained beans and pork rind with a little of their cooking water, correct the salt and cook on a low flame for about another 20 minutes.

Fegato alla veneziana

when half cooked. Add salt and pepper only when ready to serve.

Involtini al sugo
(Veal or beef rolls in tomato sauce)

There are dozens of recipes in Italy for involtini *that differ with regard to the kind of meat used, the kind of sauce they are cooked in, and the ingredients of the stuffing. The one we offer is, however, one of the most common and can be found all over Italy, so that it is difficult to determine exactly where it originated.*

Ingredients *(For 4)* :

Veal or beef	*4 slices*
Cured or cooked prosciutto	*4 slices*
Tomato puree	*5 oz (150 g)*
Dried mushrooms	*¹/₂ oz (10 g)*

One glass of Marsala wine,
  parmesan cheese, broth,
  onion, oil, butter,
  salt, pepper

Preparation:
Let the mushrooms soak in hot water

for half an hour until soft. Then squeeze the water out, cut them into large pieces and cook in a pan with a little oil, salt and pepper for about 10 minutes. Pound the slices of meat slightly and cut away any strips of fat from the edges. Lay the slices on a cutting board and sprinkle a little grated cheese on them. Then cover them with a slice of ham and some of the mushrooms. Roll up the slices of meat so that the filling does not come out and tie them or fix them with toothpicks and roll them lightly in flour. Heat 1 ounce of butter in a pan with a tablespoon of oil and brown the meat rolls on a high flame so that they turn golden on both sides. Sprinkle them with the Marsala and when this has evaporated, add salt, pepper, and the tomato puree. Cook on a very slow flame for 40-45 minutes. If the gravy dries, add a little hot broth. At the end add some chopped parsley. Untie the rolls and serve them at once.

If you cannot find...
Marsala: you can substitute dry white wine, Madera, or brandy.

Involtini al sugo

Maiale al latte
(Pork in milk)

This is a very tasty but delicate dish which uses simple ingredients and is in no way difficult to prepare. You can render the meat tenderer still if you marinate it for a few hours before cooking, covered with slices of onion, celery, and carrot and a few tablespoons of oil, brandy, and any aromatic herbs you like. You must keep it in a cool place and turn often.
Before cooking, remove the vegetables and drain well.

Ingredients *(For 4) :*
Pork loin   *2 lb   (200 g)*
Milk, flour, brandy, an onion,
  bay leaf, butter, nutmeg, salt

Preparation:
Remove any excess fat from the pork and then roll in flour.
In a pan only a little larger than the piece of meat, brown with $1^{1}/_{2}$ ounces of butter and when golden on all sides moisten with a small glass of brandy and let this evaporate.
Add the sliced onion, a bay leaf, and as much hot milk as needed to cover the piece of meat. Bring to a boil, cover and cook very slowly for an hour and 40 minutes.
Turn the meat frequently during the cooking. If the milk dries up, add a little more.
When almost done, add salt and a little grated nutmeg. Take out the bay leaf. When cooked, pass the gravy through a sieve and serve it with the meat cut in slices.

Ossibuchi alla milanese
(Milanese veal shins)

There are two main Italian recipes for cooking ossibuchi, *the cut of meat that is taken from the shin bone of the cow.*
One, which is found everywhere, but mainly in central and southern Italy, cooks the meat in a thick tomato sauce; the other, the one we present here, is one of the favorite recipes in Lombard cooking.
Its main feature is the very aromatic gremolada, *which is to say, the minced aromatic mixture that is added when the dish is cooked.*

Ingredients *(For 4) :*
4 ossibuchi (veal shins)
Parsley, garlic, flour, lemon rind,
  broth, tomato paste, butter, oil, salt,
  pepper

Preparation:
Cut the layer of fat surrounding the veal shins in 2 or 3 places so that they do not curl up during the cooking. Flour them lightly.
Brown the veal shins on a medium flame in $1^{1}/_{2}$ ounces of butter and a tablespoon of oil (the latter is only to keep the butter from burning).
When golden on both sides, moisten with a ladleful of hot broth in which a teaspoon of tomato paste has been

diluted. Cover and turn the heat down as low as possible. Cook for about an hour adding salt and pepper only towards the end.

Add a little more broth if necessary during the cooking.

A few minutes before the end, sprinkle the meat with a mixture of chopped parsley, garlic, and a piece of lemon rind.

POLLO ALLA DIAVOLA ("Devil's chicken")

This dish of Tuscan origin owes its name to the great amount of pepper used to season the chicken and which makes it quite hot.

It is a very simple recipe whose main feature lies in the way the chicken is split open, flattened as much as possible, and then grilled.

Ingredients *(For 4) :*
One chicken
Bay leaf, sage, rosemary, oil, salt, pepper

Ossibuchi alla milanese

Preparation:

Clean and prepare the chicken for cooking, then split it open from the breast, but without cutting it all the way through. Flatten the chicken with a mallet taking care not to break the bones. Mix 4 tablespoons of oil with minced herbs: a sprig of rosemary, a bay leaf, and a few sage leaves.
Brush the chicken with this aromatic oil, salt it, sprinkle with a lot of pepper and then cook on a red-hot grill or under the broiler.
Cook for 40 minutes, turning frequently and basting with the oil and herbs each time.

Pollo in umido
(Stewed chicken)

Many different recipes in different regions of Italy go by this name, but all of them indicate pieces of chicken cooked in an abundant sauce of tomato and vegetables.
One of the best-liked is the recipe we give here made with small onions.

Ingredients *(For 4) :*
A cleaned
chicken approx. 2¹/₂ lb (1 kg)
Small onions 1 lb (500 g)
Tomato pulp 10 oz (275 g)
Dried mushrooms ¹/₂ oz (15 g)
Celery, carrot, parsley, bay leaf, oil, butter, salt, pepper, broth, dry white wine

Pollo in umido

Preparation:

Soften the mushrooms in hot water for half an hour, then wash and press them slightly, but save the water. Cut the chicken into pieces. In a large pot (preferably of terracotta) heat 1 ounce of butter and 3 tablespoons of oil. Brown the chicken until it is golden on all sides, then moisten with half a glass of wine and let this evaporate. Then add a mixture of chopped celery, carrot, and parsley. Add salt, pepper, and after a few minutes the mushrooms and onions too. Strain the mushroom water well and add. When this has partially evaporated, add the tomato and a bay leaf. Cover and cook on a low flame for about 40 minutes. Stir the mixture from time to time checking to see that there is a good amount of juice until the chicken is cooked, and the gravy has become fairly thick. (If necessary add some hot broth). Correct the salt and serve.

Polpette al sugo

Polpette al sugo
(Meat balls in tomato sauce)

This dish was originally "humble folks" food since it was made from the least choice cuts of meat and even *left-overs. Italy is not the only country that makes meat balls. What makes this recipe Italian is the use of ingredients like* mortadella *and the abundant* tomato and basil sauce. Meat balls feature frequently on the tables of Italian families, and often they are eaten only fried, without the tomato sauce. Smaller ones in sauce are often used with pasta in the South. Soft mashed potatoes are perfect to accompany this recipe.

Ingredients (For 4) :

Ground beef	7 oz (200 g)
Ground veal	7 oz (200 g)
Mortadella	4 oz (100 g)
Tomato pulp	14 oz (400 g)

2 eggs
Parmesan cheese, breadcrumbs, parsley, garlic, sweet basil, oil, salt, pepper

Preparation:

Mince the *mortadella* finely and mix with the meat, the eggs, a large handful of parmesan cheese, and a spoonful of chopped parsley. Mix well and season with salt and pepper. The mixture should not be too soft. (Add a few breadcrumbs if necessary.) Make apricot-sized meatballs and flatten

them slightly, then roll them in breadcrumbs.
Fry in abundant oil (olive oil is best) on a moderate flame with a garlic clove that you will remove as soon as it turns golden. Combine the tomato, oil, a few fresh basil leaves, salt and pepper (or hot red chili pepper, if you prefer), and cook for 10 minutes on a low flame. After frying the meatballs, drain them on paper to absorb the oil and then add them to the tomato sauce. Cook on a low flame for about ten minutes.

If you cannot find...
Mortadella: use cooked *prosciutto*.
Parmesan: use another tasty grating cheese .

ROLLÈ DI VITELLO (Veal roll)

This is only one of many variations of this dish which can be made with other meats too (beef or turkey) and which can be stuffed in many different ways. The version offered here is perhaps the most common one, and there is scarcely an Italian family that does not frequently prepare this dish.

Ingredients (For 4) :

A large, lean slice of veal	1½ lb (600 g)
Spinach	9 oz (250 g)
Sliced cooked Prosciutto	4 oz (100 g)

2 eggs
Parmesan cheese, broth, oil, butter, sage, salt, pepper

Preparation:

Have your butcher cut a slice of veal that is wide and thin enough to be stuffed and rolled. Flatten it with a wet mallet and season with salt and pepper. Beat the eggs with salt, pepper, and a tablespoon of parmesan (or any other grated cheese). Fry in butter on both sides to make a thin omelette. Cook the spinach in very little salted water, squeeze dry, and cook for a few minutes with butter. Spread the spinach, the *prosciutto* and the omelette on the slice of veal, roll the meat up tightly from one of the long ends and tie it with white string. Brown the meat roll in a pan with a little butter and 2-3 tablespoons of oil and a few sage leaves. When it has browned on all sides, moisten with the hot broth and cook on a very low flame for about an hour. Towards the end add salt and pepper. Add more hot broth, if necessary.

When cooked, untie and let the meat cool for 10 minutes then slice, though not too thinly. Serve in its sauce.

Rollè di vitello

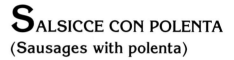

SALSICCE CON POLENTA
(Sausages with polenta)

This hearty winter dish is eaten everywhere from northernmost Italy to Tuscany. Polenta is much less used elsewhere in Italy where mashed potatoes or simply bread replace it. For cooking polenta, see the recipe in the recipe section "Appetizers."

Ingredients *(For 4)* :

Yellow polenta	*11 oz*	*(300 g)*
Sausages	*11 oz*	*(300 g)*
Tinned beans	*14 oz*	*(400 g)*
Tinned tomato pulp	*1 lb*	*(500 g)*
Bacon	*3 oz*	*(80 g)*

White or red wine, celery,
  a carrot, an onion, bay leaf,
    parsley, olive oil,
      salt, pepper

Preparation:

Finely chop a stalk of celery, a carrot, an onion, and the bacon. Brown this mixture in a pan (preferably of terracotta) with 3-4 tablespoons of oil.
After a few minutes add the sausages pierced with a fork so that they do not split open and let them brown slightly on all sides.

Moisten with half a glass of wine and let this evaporate, then add the tomato, a bay leaf, pepper and a little salt.
Cover the pan and cook for about half an hour. Uncover, add the well-drained beans, and cook for another 15 minutes.

There should be a lot of quite thick sauce. If necessary, add some hot broth or water during the cooking. Sprinkle with parsley. Serve the sausages and sauce on the polenta which you should have prepared in the meantime.

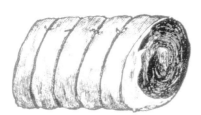

Saltimbocca alla romana

The curious name of this dish probably comes from the fact that the meat is cut into quite small pieces that hence can "pop" into your mouth (saltimbocca) and be eaten in one bite. In any case it is an example of the easy-going imagination of the Romans. The best cut of meat for this dish is veal rump, which will cut into slices having the best shape and size for saltimbocca.

Ingredients *(For 4) :*

Sliced lean veal	14 oz	(400 g)
Cured prosciutto		
thinly sliced	3 oz	(80 g)

Saltimbocca alla romana

Sage, flour, butter, oil, dry white wine,
    salt, pepper

Preparation:
Cut the meat into regular, not very
large pieces, and remove any fat
around the edges. Flatten the meat
slightly with a mallet, roll it in flour
and place a slice of *prosciutto* and a
sage leaf on each piece, fastening with
a toothpick. Heat 1 ounce of butter and
a tablespoon of oil in a wide frying
pan, then brown the pieces of
saltimbocca over a high flame, first on
the meat side and then the ham side.
Sprinkle on a little wine, letting it
evaporate on a high flame then add salt
and pepper. Serve at once with the
sauce that forms.

If you cannot find...
Cured *prosciutto*: use cooked ham.

Scaloppine ai funghi
(Veal escalope with mushrooms)

*It is difficult to establish the origin of
this recipe. Simple and fast to make,*

Scaloppine ai funghi

*one finds it everywhere and almost all
restaurants feature it. Although it is
commonly made with simple cultivated
mushrooms, the dish gains a great
deal if one can use choice mushrooms
only just gathered.*

Ingredients *(For 4)* :

Sliced veal	*1 lb (500 g)*
Mushrooms	*10 oz (300 g)*
Mozzarella	*4 oz (100 g)*

Parsley, flour, oil, butter, salt, pepper,
  dry white wine

Preparation:
Clean the mushrooms, slice them not
too thinly and sauté on a high fire in
4 tablespoons of oil with a crushed
garlic clove. Add salt and pepper and
cook for about 15 minutes. Sprinkle on

some minced parsley. Pound the meat slightly, roll in flour and brown it in a wide pan with 1 ounce (30 g) of butter. As soon as it turns color moisten with 2 tablespoons of wine, then add salt and pepper and lower the flame. Add the mushrooms and continue cooking for 5-8 minutes. Cover each *scaloppina* with a thin slice of mozzarella, remove from the heat and serve.

Scaloppine al Marsala
(Veal with Marsala)

Among the many recipes for veal scaloppine *that one finds in Italy, this is one of the classics. Instead of Marsala one can use a somewhat similar wine such as Madeira or dry sherry, but the dish will lose its Italian character. Another good version of this dish substitutes plain dry white wine for the Marsala, but it doesn't have nearly so distinctive an aroma.*

Ingredients *(For 4)* :
Slices of lean

Spezzatino con piselli

veal   1 lb (500 g)
A liqueur glass of Marsala wine, flour,
   butter, parsley, salt, pepper

Preparation:
Flatten the meat slightly and cut into
regular, not too large pieces.
Roll these lightly in flour. Heat
2 ounces of butter in a wide pan and
brown the meat on both sides over a
high flame.
Add salt and pepper and moisten with
the Marsala.
When ready, sprinkle with some
chopped parsley and serve.

Spezzatino
CON PISELLI
(Beef stewed with peas)

*This is one of many versions of a dish
commonly found all over Italy –
chunks of meat, generally beef or veal,
stewed in a sauce, sometimes with
potatoes or other vegetables.*
*The version with peas is a classic and
the recipe we offer here is particularly
representative of Tuscan and central*

Italian cuisine in general.

Ingredients *(For 4)* :
Lean stewing beef   1½ lb (600 g)
Shelled peas
  (fresh or frozen)   7 oz (200 g)
Tinned tomato pulp   11 oz (300 g)
Half an onion, robust red wine,
  garlic, parsley, fresh basil,
  olive oil, salt,
  pepper

Preparation:
Heat 4 tablespoons of oil in a
terracotta pot and brown a mixture of
minced onion, a garlic clove and a
small bunch of parsley.
After a few minutes add the beef and
brown it on all sides. Moisten with
half a glass of wine and let it
evaporate.
Then add the tomato, a few basil
leaves, salt, pepper, and simmer for
about 2 hours on a very low flame.
Add a little hot water from time to
time if needed.
During the last half hour add the peas
and correct the salt.

Trippa alla parmigiana
(Tripe parmesan)

*Tripe (the stomach lining of grazing
animals) is one of the most rustic of all
Italian dishes, and also one of the
most tasty.*
*Other countries, however, do not
always appreciate tripe, so it may
sometimes not be easy to find.*
*If you can, however (perhaps ordering
it from your butcher), it is worth trying
this recipe, which is probably the
favorite way of making it in Italy.*

Ingredients *(For 4)* :
Pre-cleaned tripe   2 lb (1 kg)
Grated parmesan   4 oz (100 g)
Tinned tomatoes   14 oz (400 g)
2 medium-sized onions
Dry white wine, broth, olive oil,
  salt, pepper

Preparation:
Slice the onions very thin and cook
them in a pot (preferably terracotta)
with about half a glass of oil, but
without letting them brown.

Trippa alla parmigiana

Vitello tonnato
(Veal in tuna sauce)

This Piedmontese dish may have come from France, but today it is very widely found all over Italy, where it is prepared not only at home, but in rosticcerie *and even in the delicatessen departments of supermarkets.*
As well as a main course this dish can be served as an appetizer and is particularly suitable in summer.
Lean and regular slices of veal should be used. The dish can also be prepared several hours in advance – in fact, the flavor will thus be improved – but it is necessary to cover in aluminum foil so that the sauce does not dry out   and, of course, it should be kept refrigerated.

Ingredients *(For 4)* :

A lean piece of veal	*2 lb*	*(1 kg)*
Mayonnaise	*3-4 tablespoons*	
Tuna in oil (drained)	*11 oz*	*(300 g)*
2-3 anchovies under oil		
Capers	*1 tablespoon*	
Celery, carrot, onion, parsley, salt, peppercorns		

Add the tripe cut into strips and cook on a low flame for a few minutes. Moisten with a glass of wine, and when this has evaporated, add the tomato and bring once more to a boil. Then add a few ladles of hot broth and cook on a very low flame for about 2 ½ hours.
Check occasionally to see that it is not too dry, and add more broth if necessary.
When almost cooked, correct the salt and add pepper. Mix in half the cheese with the tripe, transfer to an oven dish and sprinkle the rest of the cheese over the top. Put into a hot oven (480°F or 250°C) for 5-6 minutes or until slightly browned on top.

Preparation:

Boil some water with the vegetables, a few sprigs of parsley, and a few peppercorns. Salt and put in the veal, tied to keep its shape.

Boil the meat for about 1 $\frac{1}{4}$ hours, then let it cool in its broth.

When cold, slice thinly. Put the tuna through a blender with the capers and anchovies, 1-2 tablespoons of the broth and some salt, if needed. Add the mayonnaise to the cream thus obtained. You should have a soft, not too thick sauce. (Add a few drops more of broth, if necessary.)

Put the veal slices on a serving dish and cover with the tuna sauce.

Garnish with a few capers and let it rest for a few minutes before serving.

Vitello tonnato

FISH

For a country like Italy, with its extensive coastline, fish has always been a prime alimentary resource. And yet until relatively recent times, the custom of eating fish was limited to the coastal areas.

For reasons connected to transport and the short conservation time of fresh fish, the only product that reached the internal areas for centuries was salted cod.

Nevertheless, particularly in the South, there is a rich repertoire of fish and seafood recipes. Many of these recipes are quite simple, and rightly so: simple cooking, with very few ingredients, will not cover up its delicate taste. But in a few cases the Italian imagination has embroidered the basic recipes in a way to create very colorful and tasty dishes which raise even the humblest denizen of the sea into a choice morsel.

Among the many recipes, we have chosen those which combine fish with the most typical flavors of the Mediterranean.

In regions particularly rich in lakes and streams, freshwater fish was also once highly appreciated, but today this is becoming rare, with the exception of trout which is bred and sold everywhere in the country.

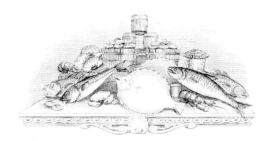

ACCIUGHE IN TORTIERA
(Baked anchovies)

Throughout the South this recipe is much used and liked, particularly in Apulia. It is a simple, "humble" dish, inasmuch as it uses a very economical kind of fish, but one of the tastiest. Besides anchovies, it can also be made with sardines.

Ingredients *(For 4) :*

Very fresh anchovies	*1 lb 2 oz*	*(600 g)*
Breadcrumbs	*4 oz*	*(100 g)*

Olive oil, a lemon, garlic, parsley, salt, pepper

Preparation:
Clean the anchovies, removing the heads and innards, then cut open and take out the spine.
Rinse and dry them. Finely chop a bunch of parsley with 2 garlic cloves and mix with the breadcrumbs.

Put half the anchovies in a baking dish and cover with half the breadcrumb mixture, the juice of half a lemon and a little oil. Make another layer in the same way. Cook in the oven for about 20 minutes at 380° F (190° C) and cool for 5 minutes before serving.

Baccalà alla Vicentina
(Stockfish Vicenza-style)

Since for many years stockfish (or salted cod) was the only kind of fish available in many Italian regions, it inspired a large number of recipes which differed considerably from one region to another. We present here one of the most famous, which takes its name from the city where it was invented (Vicenza), but which has since spread beyond the confines of its hometown. In the Veneto area it is served together with piping hot polenta.

Ingredients *(For 4)* :
Stockfish
  after soaking   *¹/₃ lb*   *(800 g)*

Milk	*1 pint (¹/₂ liter)*
Anchovy fillets in oil	*4*

Parmesan cheese, flour, parsley,
  onion, white wine, butter, olive oil,
  salt, pepper

Preparation:
Chop an onion finely and brown it in a pan with 4-5 tablespoons of oil.
Add the anchovies cut up and let them dissolve.
Then add a small bunch of minced parsley and half a glass of wine.
Cook slowly until the liquid evaporates.
At this point add the hot milk, a generous knob of butter and bring to a boil.
Correct the salt, add pepper and remove from the fire.
In the meantime remove the skin and bone the stockfish, cut it into pieces and roll in flour.
Place in a buttered baking dish (in one layer only) and sprinkle on 2-3 tablespoons of grated parmesan.
Pour on the milk sauce you have prepared and put the dish into the oven at 350° F (180° C).

When the sauce has thickened into a cream, the fish is ready to be served.

If you cannot find...
Parmesan: use a hard and tasty grating cheese.

Branzino ripieno
(Stuffed sea bass)

One of the choicest of fish, sea bass is also known as spigola, *particularly in southern and central Italy.*
It is usually cooked in a simple way, boiled, broiled or baked.
But on special occasions it may be prepared in a more elaborate way, as in the recipe we offer here, suitable for the meatless Christmas Eve table.

Ingredients *(For 4)* :
A large
sea bass   *approx. 2¹/₂ lb*   *(1 kg)*
Dried mushrooms   *¹/₂ oz*   *(10 g)*
2 lemons
Dry white wine, breadcrumbs,
  onion, parsley, olive oil, salt,
  pepper

Preparation:

Soak the mushrooms in hot water for half an hour. Clean and scale the fish, rinse and dry. Finely chop a small onion and brown it in a pan with 2 tablespoons of oil on a slow fire. After about 10 minutes add the mushrooms minced together with a small bunch of parsley.

Salt, pepper and cook slowly for 10 minutes sprinkling the mixture with a little wine.

At the end, mix in some breadcrumbs and remove from the fire. Salt and lightly pepper the inside of the fish, then stuff with the mushroom mixture.

Make some cuts in the skin on the back of the fish to allow for more uniform cooking.

Wash and slice the lemon, putting the slices on the bottom of a baking dish. Place the fish on top.

Pour the wine over the fish. Salt, pepper and moisten with a little oil, then bake in a 380°F (190°C) oven for about 40 minutes. When done, remove the lemon and pour the juices in the pan over the fish.

CALAMARI ALLA GRIGLIA
(Grilled squid)

Ingredients *(For 4) :*

Whole squid   approx. 2 lb (800 g)
Olive oil, parsley, garlic, salt, pepper

Calamari alla griglia

Preparation:

Clean the squids and prepare them for cooking. Put them in a wide and fairly deep dish. Moisten with 5-6 tablespoons of olive oil, a dash of pepper, a few slices of garlic and some parsley sprigs. Marinate, turning occasionally, for at least one hour. Then drain well and cook on a red hot grill for about 20 minutes, turning them 2-3 times. When done, salt lightly and dress with a little oil and, if you like, a few squeezes of lemon juice.

Tomato puree	14 oz (400 g)
1 egg	
Parsley, breadcrumbs,	
garlic, basil,	
lemon, capers,	
pecorino cheese,	
olive oil, salt	

Preparation:
To prepare the sauce: heat 2 tablespoons of oil in a pan with a garlic clove which you will remove as soon as it turns golden. Add the tomato puree and a few basil leaves. Let the sauce thicken for 10-15

Calamari ripieni
(Stuffed squid)

With many variations, this dish is prepared in all the Italian sea coast areas, from Liguria (where the stuffing also contains ingredients such as beet greens, pine nuts, and dried mushrooms) to Sicily (where the stuffing always uses a strong cheese such as pecorino or salted ricotta). The version we give here is closer to the southern Italian style, which is prepared not only in Sicily, but also in Campania, Calabria and Apulia, without any important differences among them.

Ingredients *(For 4)* :
4 squid   approx. 2 oz each (150 g)

Calamari ripieni

minutes on a medium flame. Clean the squid removing the ink bags, the eyes and the skin. Remove the head and tentacles.

Gently turn the squid "sacks" inside out and remove their yellowish filaments. Mince the head and tentacles finely and brown them in a pan where you have already browned a clove of minced garlic in very little oil.

After a few minutes add 4 tablespoons of breadcrumbs, the egg, a tablespoon of capers, one of chopped parsley, one of grated *pecorino*, a little lemon juice, and a pinch of hot red chili pepper. Salt this mixture and stuff the squid with it, but not too full. Sew each up with white thread. Heat the sauce in a pot (preferably of terracotta) and place the squid inside carefully, cover, and cook slowly for about 40 minutes.

If you cannot find...
Tomato puree: use 16 ounces of tinned tomatoes put through the blender.
Pecorino cheese: substitute with any strong and slightly sharp grating cheese.

Canocchie olio e limone

Canocchie Olio E Limone
(Prawns in oil and lemon)

Ingredients *(For 4) :*

Prawns	*2 ¹/₃ lb (1.2 kg)*

Parsley, garlic, bay leaf,
  lemon, dry white wine,
  oil, salt, pepper

Preparation:
Make an infusion by soaking a garlic clove in a cup of oil for 2-3 hours, then remove the garlic. Clip the legs off the prawns and rinse. Put a glass of wine and about 2 quarts of water in a pot. Add a bay leaf and a slice of lemon, salt, and some peppercorns.

Bring to a boil and add the prawns and cook on a very low flame for 3-4 minutes, then drain. Cut the prawn shells and pull out the meat without damaging it, then put in a bowl. Beat the juice of one lemon with the salt and pepper in the garlic oil. Add minced parsley and pour this dressing over the prawns. Let the flavors blend for at least an hour, then serve.

Fritto misto
(Mixed fry)

There is no seafood restaurant in Italy which doesn't feature a fritto misto *on its menu. But it is less easy to find the dish prepared as it should be. Often, in restaurants, as at home, it is prepared with frozen fish, whereas the best results, of course, are obtained with fresh ingredients. Some cooks dip the fish in an egg and flour batter before frying, whereas easier on the cook, as well as the digestion, is to use only flour as in the recipe presented here. In preparing this dish pay attention not to get burned by hot oil that can splatter on contact with the fish.*

Fritto misto

Ingredients *(For 4) :*

Small squid	*11 oz (300 g)*
Shrimp	*11 oz (300 g)*
Small anchovies	*11 oz (300 g)*

4 small mullets
A lemon, flour, oil, salt

Preparation:

Clean, rinse and dry all the sea food. Remove the ink sack, mouth, eyes, and inner bone from the squid, and detach the tentacles. Roll all the ingredients in flour and fry them in deep, very hot oil: first the mullet and the anchovies, then the squid and shrimp. Drain them when they are golden and lay them on absorbent paper for a moment. Salt and serve with lemon.

INVOLTINI DI PESCE SPADA
(Swordfish rolls)

Swordfish is caught mostly off the Sicilian and Calabrian coasts, for which reason most of the recipes for it come from these two regions.
The involtini di pesce spada *are typical of both areas with very few differences.*
Only a few simple ingredients are required, as is usually the case with Italian fish recipes.
If you want to give the dish a special touch you can decorate it with thin slices of orange or lemon, a few black olives and some whole sprigs of parsley.
Besides giving the dish a more elegant appearance, such touches immediately evoke its place of origin.

Ingredients *(For 4) :*

4 slices of		
* swordfish*	*approx. 1 lb*	*(500 g)*
Breadcrumbs	*2 oz*	*(50 g)*
Capers	*1 oz*	*(30 g)*

Parsley, garlic, lemon, olive oil,
* salt, pepper*

Slicing a swordfish

Preparation:

Make the sauce which Sicilians call *salmoriglio* by beating with a fork the juice of half a lemon with 6 tablespoons of oil and a pinch of salt. Add a sliced clove of garlic and a few whole sprigs of parsley.

Cover the sauce and let it macerate. Mince the capers with half a clove of garlic and a small bunch of parsley and mix in breadcrumbs, salt and pepper. Remove the skin from the slices of fish which should be rather wide and quite thin.

Spread some of the breadcrumb mixture on each slice, roll it up and tie with string.

Brush the slices with oil and cook them on a very hot grill.

When done, untie them and serve with the sauce.

Orata alla Pugliese
(Sea bream Apulian-style)

Among the most prized fish the Italian coast has to offer, orata is usually simply grilled to enhance its fresh flavor. In a few more elaborate recipes, however, its firm, tasty flesh is the basis of less simple, but particularly suitable recipes. This Apulian one is a good example where the orata is garnished with potatoes and cooked in the oven with particularly appetizing results.

Ingredients *(For 4) :*
2 medium sea
  bream   *approx. 2$\frac{1}{3}$ lb*   *(1 kg)*
Non-floury potatoes   *1 $\frac{1}{3}$ lb* *(600 g)*
Pecorino   *2 $\frac{1}{3}$ oz*   *(60 g)*
Garlic, parsley, lemons, olive oil,
  salt, pepper

Preparation:

Peel the potatoes, cut them into fairly thin slices, and parboil them for about 5 minutes, then let them dry on a clean cloth. Mince two large garlic cloves very finely together with a good amount of parsley. Add 8-10 tablespoons of oil to form a sauce. Clean the fish, removing their insides and scales, then rinse and dry. Oil an oven dish just big enough for the fish. Put half the potatoes in a layer on the bottom, salt and pepper them and season with a little of the sauce and half the grated *pecorino* cheese. Lay the fish over the potatoes after having seasoned them inside and out with a little of the aromatic sauce. Cover the fish with the remaining potatoes, grated cheese and salt and pepper. Pour on a little oil and roast in the oven for about half an hour at 425° F (220°C).

If you cannot find...
Pecorino: use another aged and quite strong cheese.

PESCE AI PEPERONI
(Fish with bell peppers)

This is one of the many ways which regional Italian cooks have created to prepare fish. This dish comes from the South, Campania in particular, where sea bass is used. To make it more economical, however, one can use less choice fish and the dish will remain delicious thanks to the presence of the bell peppers.

Ingredients *(For 4) :*

A large sea bass (or
*   other fish)   approx. 2 lbs   (1 kg)*
4 firm fleshy bell peppers
Fresh mixed herbs (parsley, fresh
*   basil, thyme), garlic,*
*   olive oil, salt, pepper*

Preparation:

Wash and dry the peppers then roast them on the gas flame or under the broiler until their skin is scorched. Then peel and cut the peppers into slices. Meanwhile clean and prepare the fish for cooking. In an oval pan heat 2 cloves of garlic in 6 tablespoons of oil and take them out when they have turned golden. Place the fish inside and let the flavors blend on a moderate flame, turning it over after a few minutes with the aid of 2 spatulas and taking care not to damage it. Season with salt and pepper and the chopped herbs. Cook on a moderate flame for about 40 minutes. When half done, add the strips of bell pepper and correct the salt.

Pesce ai peperoni

Pesce al pomodoro con la pasta
(Fish with tomatoes and pasta)

For making this delicious dish you can choose among the various kinds of fish suitable for stewing: small grey mullet, hake or cod, etc. Use the excellent sauce that results for the pasta (preferably the long kind such as spaghetti *or* linguine*), thus obtaining a truly complete and satisfying one-dish meal.*

Ingredients (For 4) :
Spaghetti   12 oz (350 g)
Ripe cooking tomatoes 1¹/₃ lb (600 g)
4 single-portion grey mullets
Celery, carrot, garlic, parsley,
  olive oil, hot red chili pepper

Preparation:
Clean the fish, rinse them inside too, and dry carefully.
In a pan brown a garlic clove in 4 tablespoons of oil, eliminating it as soon as it turns golden and add a mixture of chopped onion, a small bunch of parsley, some carrot and celery. Let the flavors blend, then add the seeded tomatoes cut into small pieces.
After 10 minutes, add the salt and a little hot red chili pepper then put the fish into the sauce after having seasoned them internally with salt, chopped parsley, and a little oil. Cook on a low flame for 20-25 minutes turning the fish over carefully when half cooked. Meanwhile put the pasta water on to boil. When done, remove the fish without breaking them and keep warm. Make a puree of the sauce and if it is not thick enough, put it back on a high flame for a few minutes. When the pasta is done, drain and dress with the tomato sauce. You can serve the fish together with the pasta or, better, afterwards as a second course.

Pesce in umido
(Fish stew)

Like many Italian fish dishes, this too originates as "poor man's" food. At one time dishes like this were made with not very choice kinds of fish, which became tasty nevertheless by being cooked in a sauce of tomatoes and herbs. This is also the origin of the many recipes for fish soup to be found in all the coastal areas. For the flounder indicated in the following recipe, you can substitute any other kind of fish you prefer.

Ingredients (For 4) :
Flounder fillets   approx. 1 lb (500 g)
Shrimp tails   ¹/₂ lb (250 g)
Canned tomatoes   14 oz (400 g)
One onion, parsley, fresh basil,
  garlic, olive oil, hot red chili pepper,
  salt

Preparation:
Slice the onion thinly and brown it in 6 tablespoons of oil. Cook at a low heat for about 10 minutes, then add the tomato, salt, and ground red chili pepper.
Let the sauce thicken on a high flame for about 10 minutes, then put in the fish fillets and cook for 5 minutes. Next add the shrimp tails and a mixture of finely chopped parsley

(quite a large bunch), several basil leaves, and a small clove of garlic. Cook for another 5 minutes and serve after correcting the salt.

PESCE SPADA A GHIOTTA
(Swordfish ghiotta)

This is one of the more elaborate fish recipes and comes from Sicily – particularly the area of Messina and Palermo. Here different flavors and aromas combine in sublime harmony with swordfish, including the sweetness of raisins. If swordfish is not available you can use another firm-fleshed fish. A very similar dish, also Sicilian, is made using stockfish.

Pesce spada a ghiotta

Ingredients *(For 4)* :

Swordfish slices	approx. 1 lb	(500 g)
Tinned tomatoes	14 oz	(400 g)
Green (or black) olives	2 oz	(50 g)
Raisins	1 oz	(20 g)
Capers	1 oz	(20 g)
Pine nuts	1 oz	(25 g)
Olive oil, onion, garlic,		
dry white wine, salt, pepper		

Preparation:

Soak the raisins in lukewarm water for half an hour. Finely chop a piece of onion with a garlic clove and brown in a wide pan in 5-6 tablespoons of oil for about 10 minutes. Add the fish and brown on both sides on a high flame. Moisten with a little wine and let it evaporate. Add the tomatoes, salt, pepper, and the olives with the pits

Polipetti alla Luciana

removed. Cook uncovered on a medium flame for about 10 minutes. After cooking, the juice should become quite thick.

Polipetti alla Luciana
(Little polyps alla Luciana)

This is an old Neapolitan recipe that is made all along the Campania coast and as far as Latina in Latium. In Campania they use tasty rock polyps.

Ingredients *(For 4)* :

Small polyps	2 1/3 lb (1.2 kg)
Ripe cooking	
tomatoes	1 lb (500 g)

Garlic, hot red pepper, parsley, olive oil, salt

Preparation:

Clean the polyps and put them into a terracotta pot with a small glass of oil, the chopped tomatoes with their seeds removed, minced garlic and parsley, a piece of hot red chili pepper and a pinch of salt. Close the pot with a well-fitting cover and cook on a low flame for about 40 minutes.

Then take out the polyps, keeping them warm.
Let the sauce thicken on a very high flame, then return the polyps to the pot and cook uncovered for another 5 minutes on a medium flame.

ROMBO ALLA PUGLIESE
(Flounder Apulian-style)

Yet another southern Italian recipe where the colors and flavors of vegetables combine with the savory taste of fish, creating a dish with the unmistakable mark of the Mediterranean.
The flounder can be successfully replaced by less choice and more inexpensive but just as tasty fish, as long as the right cooking time is respected that varies according to the kind of fish and, above all, its size.

Ingredients *(For 4)* :

1 flounder	*approx. 2 lb*	*(1 kg)*
Potatoes	*14 oz*	*(400 g)*
Little tomatoes	*9 oz*	*(250 g)*
Black olives	*3 oz*	*(80 g)*

Rombo alla pugliese

Parsley, garlic, breadcrumbs, olive oil, salt, pepper

Preparation:
Clean and prepare the flounder for cooking. Peel and slice the potatoes rather thinly.
Oil generously an oven dish and sprinkle a light layer of breadcrumbs over it.

Lay the fish on this after having seasoned it inside with salt, pepper, parsley, and sliced garlic.
Place the potatoes around the fish. Arrange the little tomatoes cut in half, the pitted olives, salt, pepper, minced parsley and a handful of breadcrumbs on it. Pour on a generous amount of oil and bake in a 375° F (200° C) oven for about 25 minutes.

Sarde in saòr
(Sardines saòr)

This is a typically Venetian recipe which is commonly found in other parts of Veneto as well. It has a very strong flavor and is often served with piping hot polenta.

Ingredients *(For 4)* **:**

Sardines	1 lb 14 oz (800 g)
White onions	1 lb (500 g)
Vinegar	1 pt (¹/₂ liter)
Oil, salt, pepper	

Preparation:

Remove the insides and heads from the sardines, rinse, fry them in abundant hot oil and drain. Slice the onions very thinly and brown on a very low flame in 5 tablespoons of oil. When they are soft (after about half an hour), add salt and pepper and moisten with vinegar.

Let this come to a boil and cook for about another 5 minutes.

Alternate layers of sardines, salt, pepper, and the onions with their juice in a container. When cool, cover and keep in a cool place for at least two days before serving.

Sarde in saòr

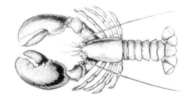

Seppie al sugo nero
(Squid in black ink)

Popular everywhere in Italy, squid are sometimes cooked in a black sauce made with their own ink. In this way they can be made into a very tasty risotto. The recipe we give here is

Venetian in origin, but with a few variations, is also common in many other regions.

Ingredients *(For 4) :*
Whole small squid   2 lb (800 g)
Dry white wine, parsley, garlic,
* onion, tomato sauce, olive oil,*
* salt, pepper.*

Preparation:
Clean the squid and save a few of the ink sacks (2 or 3). Finely chop together some onion, garlic, and quite a good amount of parsley. Brown this mixture in a terracotta pot with 4 tablespoons of oil. After 10 minutes add the squid and brown for a few minutes on a medium flame.
Moisten with half a glass of wine and, without waiting for this to evaporate entirely, add a tablespoon of tomato sauce and the ink from the ink sacks you set aside and dissolved in a little warm water. Now add salt and pepper, cover and cook slowly for about 40 minutes. Before serving, the squid should be soft and the sauce quite thick.

Seppie al sugo nero

Sogliole alla Fiorentina
(Florentine sole)

This is quite an unusual dish by Tuscan standards because of its mildness, whereas most recipes of this region have strong, decisive flavors.

Ingredients *(For 4)* :

Sole	*4 portions*
Fresh spinach	*1 1/3 lb (600 g)*
Butter	*4 oz (100 g)*
Milk, flour, garlic, salt, pepper	

Preparation:

Wash the spinach well and cook it in a pot with a little salt and no water. When cooked, press out the water and chop.

Heat the spinach in a pan with 2 ounces of butter and a crushed garlic clove. Clean the sole removing the head and the grey skin. Roll in flour and fry until golden in 2 ounces of butter that has been whipped with a crushed garlic clove. When done on both sides, salt and pepper and put in an oven dish that can be used for

Triglie alla livornese

serving, cover with the spinach and about half a glass of milk. Bake in an oven at 425° F (220° C) for about 15 minutes.

TRIGLIE ALLA LIVORNESE
(Mullet Livorno-style)

The coastal areas of Tuscany have a fish and seafood cuisine that is much different from the excellent meat and abundant vegetables eaten inland. The link between these two Tuscan culinary souls is the taste for strong and decisive flavors which also marks the fish recipes of this region. Examples are offered by two of the most famous Livornese recipes: cacciucco *(a rich and tasty fish soup) and the* triglie *recipe which follows.*

Ingredients *(For 4)* :

Rock mullet	*2 lb (1 kg)*
Tinned tomatoes	*1 lb (500 g)*
Onion, garlic, parsley,	
olive oil, flour, salt, pepper	

Preparation:
Heat 3 tablespoons of oil in a pan with a piece of sliced garlic which you will remove as soon as it is browned.

Add some minced onion to the oil and cook on a low flame for a few minutes, then add the tomato, salt and pepper. Let the sauce thicken for 10-15 minutes on a medium flame. Meanwhile clean, rinse and dry the fish. Flour lightly and fry in a pan with a lot of quite hot oil (seed oil will suffice).
Drain the fried fish and put in the pan with the tomato sauce.
Let them absorb the flavors of the sauce for 3-4 minutes on a low flame, turning them over at least once.
Correct the salt and pepper, sprinkle on some minced parsley and serve.

SIDE DISHES

These are the vegetable dishes that complete the second courses of meat, poultry, or fish. They are mostly cooked vegetables, while raw ones, served as salad or with dips, follow the second course and prepare the palate for the fruit or dessert that are still to come. Given the great variety of vegetables available in Italy in all seasons, there are countless vegetable recipes. In some cases they regard ingredients typical of certain zones that may be impossible to find in other parts of the country. For example, the *lampascioni* beloved of the Apulians is a kind of bitter onion that is found nowhere else. For obvious reasons we will stick here to the vegetables that are easy to find in all countries.

ASPARAGI ALLA PARMIGIANA
(Asparagus parmesan)

The area around Bassano del Grappa in Veneto is especially famous for the production of this choice vegetable, particularly the large, fleshy white kind. The recipe given here, one of the most common ways of preparing asparagus, can be used with any variety of this vegetable, including the more common green kind. Out of season it can also be made with frozen asparagus although its flavor is obviously inferior to the fresh. Not recommended are canned asparagus which have far too different a flavor. The recipe given here is often served with fried eggs. In this way it constitutes a light but complete second course.

Ingredients *(For 4)* :
Fresh asparagus   2 lb   (1 kg)
Parmesan cheese   4 oz   (100 g)
8 eggs (optional)
Butter, salt, pepper to taste

Preparation:
Clean the asparagus, scrape the stems and slice to make them even in length. Wash carefully (the tips are very delicate) and tie them into a bunch with white string. Boil up a lot of salted water in a high, narrow pot and place the asparagus in it vertically with the tips out of the water.
They will cook in the steam. Cook for 15-20 minutes according to the thickness of the stems. Drain and untie, then put them on a tray to let the water drain off.
Arrange the asparagus on a serving plate, season with ground pepper, butter, and grated parmesan cheese. Serve at once, or keep them warm while you fry the eggs which you will put on top of the asparagus and serve very hot.

Broccoli alla Calabrese
(Broccoli Calabrian-style)

Broccoli is a member of the cabbage family and is quite similar to cauliflower, composed as it is of small flower-like "bouquets." The difference is in their green color which is more or less dark according to the variety. They are found everywhere in Italy but are most appreciated in the southern and central regions where one finds various kinds often used in vegetable soups or in pasta sauces.

Ingredients *(For 4)* :

Green broccoli	2 lb	(1 kg)
Black olives	3 oz	(80 g)
Tinned tomatoes	5 oz	(150 g)

One medium-large onion, olive oil, salt, hot red chili pepper

Preparation:

Clean the broccoli, removing the hardest parts of the stem, then divide into clumps. Boil for 5 minutes in salted water, then drain and save some of the water. Slice the onion thinly and brown in 4-5 tablespoons of oil. When it begins to turn color add a little of the broccoli water and cook for another 15 minutes.

Then add the broccoli and let the flavors blend. Add the olives with the pits removed and cut into small pieces, the tomatoes, and a little piece of red chili pepper. Cook on a low flame for 15-20 minutes, adding, if necessary, some of the broccoli water.

When ready, the sauce must be rather dry. Correct the salt and serve.

If you cannot find...
Broccoli: you can use cauliflower instead.

Caponata

This delicious vegetable mixture is typical of some southern regions, particularly Calabria and Sicily. It is a triumph of Mediterranean flavors and is made in the summer. It is a perfect accompaniment to fish simply cooked or meat dishes, as well as eggs, cheese or cold cuts. Besides being a side dish, caponata *can be an appetizer, perhaps served on slices of toast.*

Ingredients *(For 4)* :

Eggplant	approx. 1½ lb	(600 g)
Ripe cooking tomatoes	14 oz	(400 g)
Green olives	4 oz	(100 g)
Celery		1 bunch
Capers	2 oz	(50 g)
Pine nuts		1 tablespoon
Vinegar		½ cup
Sugar		1 tablespoon

An onion, fresh basil, olive oil, salt, pepper

Preparation:

Wash and, if you like, peel the eggplant, then cut into cubes and place in a colander. Sprinkle with salt and let cook on a low flame until the eggplant is tender. Just before removing from the fire, put in some broken basil leaves.

Let the *caponata* cool and serve at room temperature.

CARCIOFI ALLA GIUDIA
(Jewish-style artichokes)

A typical Roman dish of Jewish origin. In fact, it is a specialty of the Rome Jewish community.
It is made with the large, tasty, globe artichokes grown in Latium and today you can find them in many Roman restaurants and almost all rosticcerie.
Made in this way the artichokes are an excellent side dish for meat courses, particularly lamb.
And, of course they also make a delicious appetizer.

Ingredients *(For 4) :*
8 artichokes
  (preferably large round ones)
Olive oil, lemon,
  salt, pepper

Caponata

the water drain out for an hour. Then rinse and place on a dish towel to dry. Slice the onion and brown in a pan with 5-6 tablespoons of oil. After a few minutes add the chopped celery. Let the flavors blend for a few minutes, then add the pitted olives, capers, pine nuts, and tomato, peeled, chopped and seeded. Add salt and pepper and let the sauce thicken, then add the sugar and vinegar. Meanwhile, in another pan, fry the eggplant cubes in 5-6 tablespoons of oil until golden. Add them to the tomato sauce and

Preparation:
Clean the artichokes, removing the outside leaves, the pointed tips, and part of the stem, leaving about 2 inches (5 centimeters) which you must peel. Carefully open the leaves slightly and immerse the artichokes in cold water with the juice of one lemon for 10-15 minutes. Drain and dry. Heat about one glass of oil in a deep pot and put in the artichokes head down and very close to each other. Cook for about 20 minutes or until tender. Add salt and pepper and serve very warm.

CARCIOFI ALLA ROMANA
(Roman-style artichokes)

This dish too comes from Latium, but unlike the preceding one it is not of Jewish origin. It is, however, one of the most traditional ways of cooking the big delicious artichokes grown in the region.
Only a few ingredients are needed to make this dish, and among them is one that is also native to Latium:
mentuccia, *a kind of mint with round leaves. In many other regions artichokes are prepared in a similar way to this, but seasoned only with garlic and parsley.*

Ingredients *(For 4)* :
8 artichokes
  (preferably large round ones)
2 anchovy fillets in oil
Garlic, fresh mint, parsley,
  olive oil, lemon,
  salt, pepper

Preparation:
Clean the artichokes in the way indicated in the preceding recipe, then soak them in water and lemon juice. Mince the anchovies with 2 garlic cloves, a small bunch of parsley and the leaves of 2 mint sprigs.
Blend this mixture with salt, pepper, and 2 tablespoons of oil and fill the artichokes after spreading the leaves carefully open.
Put the artichokes, heads down, in a deep pot and close together.
Add 2-3 tablespoons of oil and about 2 glasses of warm water. Cook on a moderate flame until tender.

CIPOLLINE IN AGRODOLCE
(Sweet-and-sour onions)

Although sweet-and-sour is not a very common flavor in Italian cooking, this is the most typical way of cooking small onions.
The recipe originates in parts of Lombardy and Piedmont and makes a fine accompaniment to boiled, roasted or braised meats.

Ingredients *(For 4)* :
Small peeled onions   1 1/3 lb (600 g)
Vinegar, sugar, butter,
  olive oil, salt

Preparation:
Cook the onions for 5 minutes in slightly salted boiling water and drain. In a wide pan melt 2 ounces of butter in 2 tablespoons of oil and brown the onions on a low flame until golden, turning them carefully from time to time. Mix 2 tablespoons of vinegar with 2 of sugar and pour this on the onions. Stir and cook for another 2-3 minutes. Correct the salt and serve.

Cipolline in agrodolce

FAGIOLI ALL'UCCELLETTO
(Beans *uccelletto*)

In past centuries beans were called "the meat of the poor," during *times when meat was considered a luxury in Europe. That is why popular Italian cuisine also contains many recipes for this nutritious legume. The most common recipes are those in* *which the beans are cooked in a tomato sauce. In the North, this dish was usually served with a hot polenta. Often beans cooked this way are still eaten today with a hearty dish of pork (sausages and/or ribs). The following recipe comes from Tuscany, but under different names and with slight variations it is prepared almost everywhere in Italy.*

Ingredients *(For 4) :*

Fresh white beans	*2 lb*	*(1 kg)*
Tinned tomatoes	*11 oz*	*(300 g)*
Sage, rosemary, garlic, olive oil, salt, pepper		

Preparation:

Shell the beans and boil them in water with a sprig of rosemary, a clove of garlic, a little oil and, when they are almost done, a little salt.
Drain the beans when they are still quite firm.
Heat half a glass of oil in a pot, preferably of terracotta, and brown a garlic clove in this, then remove it.
Add the beans to the pot with a few sage leaves and, after a few moments,

Fagioli all'uccelletto

the tomato. Correct the salt, add pepper and cook on a moderate flame until the sauce thickens.

Finocchi al gratin
(Fennel au gratin)

Although this vegetable is usually eaten raw, it is often prepared au gratin. In this case there is also a simpler and lighter recipe which consists in boiling the fennel and putting it in the oven covered with breadcrumbs, grated parmesan and dabs of butter.
The recipe that follows is more elaborate and can be eaten not only as a side dish, but even as a light second course, in which case we suggest increasing the amount of cheese.

Ingredients *(For 4) :*
4 medium-large fennels
Bechamel sauce   9 oz (250 g)
Breadcrumbs, butter,
* parmesan cheese,*
* salt, pepper*

Preparation:

Clean the fennels and cut into quarters, then boil them in salted water for 5 minutes.

Drain well and put them into a pan with 2 ounces of butter until they are slightly browned.

Then put into an oven dish, cover with the bechamel to which you have added 4 tablespoons of grated parmesan, and sprinkle with a mixture of breadcrumbs and parmesan cheese (a tablespoon). Put into a hot oven until a golden crust has formed on top.

If you cannot find...
Parmesan: use emmenthal or any other grated cheese.

Fiori di zucca fritti
(Fried squash flowers)

The delicate squash flowers appear on market stalls in late spring, around June.

They are used in risotto *and pasta sauces, but are primarily eaten stuffed, or fried in batter.*

They are usually served as an appetizer, but made according to the recipe below, also make an excellent side dish for meat and fish.

What counts is to eat them as soon as they are cooked so that they are always crunchy.

Ingredients *(For 4) :*
12 very fresh squash flowers
Flour   4 tablespoons
Seed oil, salt, pepper

Preparation:

Mix the flour with a little oil and as much water as needed to obtain a liquid batter (about 5 tablespoons).

Let it rest for an hour.

Wash and dry the squash flowers very

Fiori di zucca fritti

carefully, making sure not to damage them.

Dip them in the batter so that they are well covered inside and out. Put them a few at a time in deep, hot oil and fry them on a moderate flame until the batter turns golden.

Add salt and pepper only when serving.

Melanzane al funghetto
(Eggplant *funghetto*)

Eggplant is one of the favorite vegetables in Italy. It is eaten a lot mostly in the South, and there are many recipes for making eggplant in Campania, Apulia and Sicily in particular. The following recipe comes from Campania, but it is made everywhere because it also serves as a base for other dishes (pasta sauces, filling for omelette or savory pies, etc.) It is very simple and makes an excellent side dish for meat, fish, and eggs.

Melanzane al funghetto

Ingredients *(For 4) :*

Eggplant	1³/4 lb (700 g)
Tinned tomato	9 oz (250 g)
Garlic, parsley, olive oil, salt, pepper	

Preparation:

Wash the eggplant well. Peel them, if you like. This is not essential but reduces the cooking time. Cut the eggplant into small cubes and place them in a colander. Salt and let the water drain out for at least half an hour. Heat half a glass of oil in a wide pan. Brown 2 garlic cloves in the oil. When they are golden remove. Rinse and dry the eggplant and put the cubes in the pan. Cook on a low flame for about 10 minutes, then add the tomato, some finely chopped parsley, salt if needed, and pepper. Cook for about another 20 minutes, until the sauce has thickened, and serve.

MELANZANE ALLA PARMIGIANA
(Eggplant parmesan)

This dish is sometimes confused with the more famous Eggplant Parma (see the section "Appetizers") which is a much more complete dish suitable as an appetizer or a second course. Instead Eggplant parmesan is almost exclusively vegetable and so makes a good side dish. It is easy to prepare, though remember that the eggplant must be left under salt for an hour before cooking. It is excellent either cold or hot, but at its best when just warm.

Ingredients *(For 4)* :

Eggplant	2 lb	(1 kg)
Tinned tomato	1³/₄ lb	(700 g)
Grated parmesan cheese	5 oz	(150 g)

Olive oil, seed oil, fresh sweet basil, garlic, salt, pepper

Preparation:

Peel the eggplant and cut into slices. Place them on a cutting board and salt each layer. Tilt the board so that the water will run off. Let it rest this way for an hour. Meanwhile prepare a tomato sauce with 2 tablespoons of olive oil, 2 garlic cloves, and a few basil leaves. Add salt and pepper and when all the water has evaporated, remove from the fire. Rinse, dry, and fry the eggplant, a few slices at a time in deep, hot, seed oil. When the eggplant is soft, drain and place on oil absorbing paper. Then put into an oven dish alternating with layers of tomato sauce and cheese. The last layer should be tomato and cheese. Bake in a 350° F (180° C) oven for about 30 minutes.

MELANZANE IMBOTTITE
(Stuffed eggplant)

Italian recipes for stuffing eggplant are countless (meat, vegetables, cheese and other ingredients are used). We have chosen a Neapolitan one with an almost entirely vegetable filling which makes an excellent side dish for meat. Of course one can vary it by adding a little chopped mozzarella or prosciutto, or mushrooms, or anything else your imagination might suggest.

Ingredients *(For 4)* :

2 large eggplants		
3-4 ripe cooking tomatoes		
Green olives	2 oz	(50 g)
Capers	1 oz	(25 g)

A red or yellow bell pepper, breadcrumbs, garlic, oregano, grated parmesan cheese, oil, salt, hot red chili pepper

Preparation:

Wash the eggplants and cut them in half lengthways. Scrape out the pulp with a spoon, but leave about a quarter inch of the pulp in place so that they have a boat-like shell. Salt the insides of the eggplant and turn upside down for an hour to let their water drain off. Cut the pulp into little cubes and place on a strainer.
Salt them and let rest for at least half an hour so that the water is drawn off. Brown 2 garlic cloves in about half a glass of oil, then discard the garlic when it has turned color.

Add the eggplant cubes (after draining and drying them) and after a few moments the coarsely chopped olives and capers, the peeled and seeded, chopped tomatoes, the bell pepper washed and cut into very small squares.

Season with salt, a little oregano and powdered red chili pepper, and cook for about 10 minutes on a medium flame until the water from the tomatoes has evaporated. Mix in 2 tablespoons of breadcrumbs and one of grated parmesan.

Scald the eggplant shells in salted boiling water for 2-3 minutes, then dry them well and fill with the prepared mixture. Place the stuffed eggplant in an oiled oven dish, sprinkle some breadcrumbs over the top and a drop of oil.

Bake in a 350° F (180° C) oven for about 40 minutes. They can be served hot, warm or cold.

Melanzane imbottite

PATATE AL FORNO
(Roast potatoes)

Although this dish is certainly not exclusively Italian, the potatoes get an Italian flavor by usually being seasoned with some of the most typically Italian herbs. Here is a nice variation of the universal way of cooking potatoes.

Ingredients *(For 4)* :

Potatoes	*2 lb (1 kg)*

Garlic, sage, rosemary, olive oil,
  salt, pepper

Preparation:

Peel the potatoes and cut them into pieces of the same size.

Pour about half a glass of oil into the roasting pan and heat 2 cloves of chopped garlic in the oil. Then take the pan out of the oven and mix the potatoes in with the oil. Return to the oven and roast at 480° F (250° C) for 20 minutes. Stir the potatoes carefully and add a good amount of minced rosemary and sage. Return to the oven for another 20-30 minutes, stirring from time to time. Take care not to break the potatoes. Do not salt them until 5-10 minutes before they are cooked. Add pepper. They should be well browned and crispy.

Peperonata
(Bell peppers)

This is a delicious dish which, with some variations, is prepared almost everywhere in Italy during the summer. Some recipes call for a few potatoes cut into pieces. It is excellent either hot or at room temperature.

Ingredients *(For 4)* **:**
4 bell peppers of various colors
8 cooking tomatoes
2 onions
Fresh basil, olive oil, salt, pepper

Preparation:
Slice the potatoes thin, then brown them in a pan with about half a glass of oil. As soon as they begin to turn color, add the other ingredients cut into pieces. Stir, add salt and pepper

Patate al forno

Peperonata

and a few basil leaves. Cover and cook slowly for about an hour. If at the end they are still too soupy, remove the lid and raise the flame to thicken. *Peperonata* can be served hot or cold.

If you cannot find...
Cooking tomatoes (the plum-shaped ones) fresh, use the canned variety.

Peperoni all'acciuga
(Bell peppers with anchovies)

Among the many ways of making peppers, this is an imaginative and very appetizing way that is found in several southern Italian regions and is similar in its ingredients to a Piedmontese recipe. This latter differs mainly in that instead of being rolled up, the peppers are served in strips with a sauce of anchovies, garlic, and other ingredients.

Ingredients *(For 4)* :
4 red and yellow bell peppers
2 anchovies under salt
Capers   *2 oz   (50 g)*

Bread without crust   *2 oz*   *(50 g)*
Pine nuts, parsley, garlic, olive oil,
    salt, pepper

Preparation:
Wash and dry the peppers and roast them under the broiler or over a gas flame. When the peels are burnt, rub them off, then cut the peppers open and remove the seeds and white pulp. Cut each pepper into 4 strips. Rinse the salt from the anchovies and mince them together with a small bunch of parsley, a tablespoon of pine nuts, and the capers. Mix this with the bread which has been soaked in water and squeezed dry. Season with pepper, a little salt, and a little oil. Spread the mixture on the strips of pepper and roll them up. Fix them with toothpicks and put them into an 350° F (180° C) oven for about 20 minutes. Serve hot, at room temperature, or cold.

Peperoni all'acciuga

PISELLI AL PROSCIUTTO
(Peas with *prosciutto*)

This is one of the most classic dishes to accompany scaloppine *and other meat courses. It is certainly the most usual way of preparing peas in Italy. In Latium they use bacon or* guanciale *instead of cooked ham (*prosciutto cotto*).* Guanciale *comes from the inside of the pig's mouth and is similar to Italian bacon. In other parts of Italy cured ham (*prosciutto crudo*) is used. When peas are not in season, frozen ones are widely used.*

Ingredients *(For 4) :*
Fresh shelled peas   *1½ lb*   *(600 g)*
A single slice of
prosciutto cotto   *4 oz*   *(100 g)*

Piselli al prosciutto

*A large onion, butter, olive oil,
broth, salt, pepper*

Preparation:

Slice the onion thinly and brown it in a pan with 2 ounces of butter and 2 tablespoons of olive oil on a very low flame. As soon as it begins to turn color add the *prosciutto* cut into small squares and, after a few moments, the peas. Stir to let the flavors blend then moisten with half a glass of hot broth. Salt and pepper moderately then cover and cook on a low flame for about half an hour. If necessary add some more hot broth now and then, keeping in mind that when done, the peas must be tender and dry.

RADICCHIO TREVISANO ALLA GRIGLIA
(Grilled *radicchio* Treviso)

Trevisan radicchio *is a red salad leaf. The heads are rather tapered and pointed. It has a unique, pleasantly bitter flavor. Like all lettuce leaves, it can be eaten raw.*
In its native region, Veneto, radicchio *is also grilled or steamed and used in pasta fillings, etc.*
In recent years the recipes for cooked radicchio *have passed beyond the borders of Veneto and become common all over Italy. The recipe we propose here is among the most typical and popular.*

Ingredients *(For 4)* :
Red radicchio   8 heads
Garlic, olive oil, salt, pepper

Preparation:

Clean the *radicchio*, removing the

roots which are very bitter, and any damaged outer leaves. Wash well and cut each head into two parts. Dry well. Put a good glass of oil in a wide, deep dish with a sliced garlic clove. Stir the *radicchio* in this oil for a while, then let it drain and put it in a hot pan for about 10 minutes, turning it over a few times during the cooking. A little before it is finished, add salt and pepper.

If the *radicchio* tends to dry out too much, brush with a little oil.

If you cannot find...
Radicchio: use Belgian endives.

Radicchio trevisano alla griglia

ZUCCHINE ALL'ACETO
(Zucchini in vinegar)

This is a typical southern Italian recipe where it is known as zucchine a scapece *or* scabece. *It is prepared a few hours in advance so that the vegetable can absorb the flavor of the vinegar. An equally good version is broiled zucchini.*
In either case, it is an excellent dish to accompany meats.

Ingredients *(For 4)* :
Small tender
*   zucchine*   *1³/4 lb (700 g)*
White wine vinegar   *1 glass*
Garlic, oil, salt, hot red chili pepper

Preparation:
Wash the zucchini and cut off the ends, then slice lengthways. Put on a cutting board, salt, and let the water drain off for half an hour. Then rinse and dry them. Fry the zucchini in deep hot oil and place them on paper to absorb the excess oil. Then arrange in layers in a deep, wide dish. Dress each layer with salt, red chili pepper, and

Zucchine all'aceto

sliced garlic. Pour on warmed vinegar and let the dish rest for a few hours. Serve at room temperature after draining off the vinegar.

Zucchine alla menta
(Zucchini with mint)

Zucchini are often made trifolati – *that is to say, with garlic, parsley, and oil. The recipe we offer is a variation that is mostly followed in regions of central Italy and is more aromatic because of the use of mint and fresh basil. These herbs should be shredded by hand, so as not to lose their fragrance.*

Ingredients *(For 4) :*
Small, tender
* zucchini   1³/4 lb (700 g)*
Garlic, fresh mint and basil, olive oil,
* salt, pepper*

Preparation:
Wash the zucchini, cut off the ends, and slice them, but not too thinly.
In a wide pan, heat a garlic clove in 6-7 tablespoons of oil. Remove the

garlic when it turns golden. Add the zucchini, and stir well for 2 minutes so that they take on the flavor, then add salt and pepper, cover and cook for about half an hour. Stir the zucchini from time to time and if necessary add a little hot water. During the last 5 minutes toss in a generous amount of mint and basil leaves, broken into pieces by hand.

Zucchine alla menta

(Composition created by chef Antonio Sciullo)

SWEETS AND DESSERTS

If family meals on ordinary days generally end with fresh fruit, holiday menus or formal occasions always require a "sweet" conclusion with ice cream or pastry of some sort.

At one time, sweets and desserts for most people were a luxury reserved only for important holidays.

That is why the Italian tradition is particularly rich in sweets connected with the principal holidays (Christmas, Easter, Carnival, Saints days, etc.). In most cases they are simple sweets and desserts made of basic ingredients (flour, eggs, honey or sugar, and butter).

Often they are cookies in all forms, soft coffee cakes, or old-fashioned pies.

In other cases, however, tradition has given us recipes enriched with such ingredients as *ricotta*, raisins, chocolate and fruit.

In recent decades there has been a gradual increase all over Italy of a particular type of dessert usually called "spoon desserts" because of their soft, creamy consistency.

To this category belong the puddings, "Bavarians" (a soft custard-filled pastry), and some more typically Italian desserts like *panna cotta* (cream custard), *zuppa inglese* (very Italian despite the name "English soup") and the by now very famous *Tirami su* (meaning "give me a boost"). It has not been an easy task to choose among the many Italian sweets, but the ones we have selected are decidedly among the best and most representative of Italian cuisine.

Biscotti all'anice
(Anise cookies)

Among the anise-flavored cookies that abound, one of the most famous is this Tuscan version called Brigidini *because, it appears, they were invented in the Convent of St. Brigid in Pistoia.*

Ingredients *(For 4)* :

Flour	1 1/8 cups	(150 g)
Sugar	1/2 cup	(100 g)
Anise seeds	3 oz	(75 g)
3 eggs		

Preparation:
Crush the anise seeds. Make a dough of the flour, sugar, eggs and anise seeds.
When the dough is well blended and firm let it rest for an hour, then divide into walnut-size pieces.
Roll them out wafer-thin with a floured rolling pin.

Biscotti all'anice

Oil a cookie sheet and bake in a 350° F (180° C) oven for a few minutes until they turn golden.

CASSATA SICILIANA

The Sicilian dessert tradition is perhaps the most varied and refined in Italy.
Cassata is one of the most elaborate and sumptuous of Sicilian desserts.
It is decorated with white icing and whole or sliced candied fruits.
Sicilian pastry chefs produce true masterpieces of decoration.
This dessert is very sweet, and should be eaten very fresh to appreciate the delicate flavor of the ricotta cream filling (see the section "Cheeses").
In order to shorten the time required to make this cake, we suggest buying a commercial sponge cake.

Ingredients *(For 4) :*

Sponge cake	*7 oz*	*(200 g)*
Very fresh ricotta	*9 oz*	*(250 g)*
Granulated sugar	*¹/2 cup*	*(100 g)*
Powdered sugar	*¹/2 cup*	*(100 g)*

Apricot jam	4 oz	(100 g)
Bitter chocolate	2 oz	(50 g)
Shelled pistachio nuts	1 oz	(25 g)

Candied fruits (tangerines, squash, orange, cherries) maraschino cherry liqueur, orange flower water, vanilla

Preparation:

Remove the outside crust of the sponge cake and cut it into slices. Put half of this into a cake dish lined with oiled paper.

Moisten the cake with a few spoons of maraschino.

Stir the *ricotta* vigorously with the granulated sugar and a liqueur glass of maraschino, then add the broken pieces of chocolate, the coarsely chopped pistachios with their skins removed, and 2 tablespoons of candied fruit cut into small cubes. Spread this mixture on the sponge cake and cover with the remaining slices of cake moistened with a little maraschino. Place in the refrigerator for 2-3 hours.

In the meantime mix the powdered sugar with 2 tablespoons of orange flower water so as to obtain a thick spreadable frosting (add very little water, if necessary). Put the jam through a sieve and heat it in a pan with a little water so as to obtain a gelatine. Spread this on the top and sides of the cake which you will have turned onto a plate. Then spread the frosting on the top and sides with a spatula. Let the frosting dry out, then decorate with the candied fruit (a whole tangerine, cherries, slices of orange and squash). Keep in the refrigerator and serve the same day.

If you cannot find...

Ricotta: substitute cottage cheese or any other fresh cheese that is creamy and sweet tasting.

Maraschino: use another sweet fruit liqueur.

Orange flower water: use filtered lemon juice.

Pistachios: they can be omitted.

CASTAGNACCIO

A typical example of a "humble" dessert, this is a very old recipe from Tuscany where it is still very popular. Today many people add a little sugar, but the original recipe did not call for this once very expensive ingredient. To give a slightly sweet taste to this rustic cake some raisins were used in addition to the main ingredient: chestnut flour. This was very inexpensive due to the abundance of chestnuts in the woods of the Apennines.

Ingredients (For 4) :

Chestnut flour	2 1/4 cups	(300 g)
Sugar	1/4 cup	(50 g)
Raisins	1/4 cup	(50 g)
Pine nuts	2 oz	(50 g)
Olive oil		

Preparation:

Soak the raisins in water. Put the chestnut flour into a bowl and add the sugar and about 2 glasses of water. Stir until a smooth, liquid batter is obtained. Add the pine nuts and the raisins drained and dried. Oil a wide, round, and low oven pan (*Castagnaccio* must not be more than about one inch high). Pour in the batter and cover the top with 2 tablespoons of oil. Bake in a 390° F (200° C) oven for about an hour until a thin crust is formed.

CIAMBELLINE LIEVITATE
(Doughnuts)

We have chosen this recipe among the many available because it is one of the simplest and most typical of its kind. It is native to Apulia. This kind of pastry is ever more rarely made at home because it is not a quick preparation and, above all, is easy to buy in bakeries, pastry or food shops.

Ingredients *(For 4)* :

Bread dough	*4 oz (100 g)*
Sugar	*1/2 cup (100 g)*
Boiled potatoes	*4 oz (100 g)*
Butter	*3 1/2 tablespoons*
4 eggs	
Flour	

Ciambelline lievitate

Preparation:
Sieve the potatoes and mix with the bread dough, the butter (less 1 tablespoon which you will set aside), the sugar, and the whole eggs. Knead vigorously and make a ball of the dough. Cover with a cloth and let it rise for 24 hours at room temperature (tepid). Divide the dough into pieces about 4 inches long and the width of a finger.
Form these into doughnuts and put them on a cookie sheet floured and greased with the remaining butter. Bake in a 350° F (180° C) oven until golden.

CREMA DI MASCARPONE
(Mascarpone cream)

Mascarpone *is a very creamy, fat cheese with a sweet, buttery flavor. It is native to Lombardy, and because highly perishable, it was not to be found outside that region until a few decades ago. Now, of course, it can be found anywhere in Italy, also because it is the main ingredient of what is* becoming the national dessert: Tirami su *(see the following pages).*

Ingredients *(For 4) :*
Mascarpone	
(or similar)	*14 oz (350 g)*
Powdered sugar	*³/4 cup (150 g)*
2 whole eggs plus 2 egg yolks	
Any liqueur you prefer (rum, cognac, etc.), dry cookies or wafers, salt	

Preparation:
Beat the 2 egg yolks (which must be very fresh) with the sugar. When they have become a foamy cream, add the *mascarpone,* stirring it well to remove any lumps. Add 2-3 tablespoons of

liqueur. Whip the egg whites to a peak with a pinch of salt and blend into the cream carefully. Do not stir, but fold from bottom to top. Divide the cream into 4 cups. Keep the cream in the refrigerator for an hour before serving with light cookies or wafers.

If you cannot find...
Mascarpone: use cottage cheese or cream cheese, etc.

CREMA FRITTA
(Fried cream)

This sumptuous dessert is typical of several northern regions (Lombardy, Piedmont, Veneto). It is also sometimes served together with other fried foods as a rich and elaborate between-meal snack, the "mixed fry." Preparing fried cream is not quick, but it is not difficult either. It can be an alternative to Carnival pancakes.

Ingredients *(For 4) :*
Flour	*1 ¹/8 cup (150 g)*
Sugar	*¹/2 cup (100 g)*

Milk   1 ¹/₂ pt (³/₄ liter)
4 eggs
Breadcrumbs, one large lemon
  (or else vanilla), seed oil for frying

Preparation:

Beat one whole egg and 3 yolks with the sugar until they are light and foamy. Add the flour and the grated lemon rind (or a packet of vanilla). Mix well, then add the hot milk a little at a time and stir carefully so as not to form lumps. Cook the cream on a medium flame until it is thick and entirely blended and no longer tastes of flour.

Turn the cooked cream onto a slightly oiled tray and level it out to a thickness of about ³/₄ inch and let it cool. Then cut it into squares or rectangles.

Roll these pieces in the egg white and then the breadcrumbs so that they are entirely covered on both sides.

Heat a large amount of oil in a pan and fry the slices of cream, a few at a time, until they are golden on both sides. Serve hot and sprinkled with more sugar, if you like.

CREMA PASTICCERA
(Pastry cream)

Called by this name because it is, in fact, the cream most often used for filling cakes, cream puffs, and many other pastries. It is, however, excellent also when eaten hot or cold by itself, or together with cookies. Usually it is flavored with lemon rind, but vanilla can be substituted, or a liqueur, according to taste.

Ingredients (For 4) :

Milk   1 pt (¹/₂ liter)
Flour   ¹/₃ cup   (50 g)
sugar   ³/₄ cup   (150 g)
4 egg yolks
Grated lemon rind, salt

Preparation:

Beat the egg yolks with the sugar until foamy and light in color. Add the flour, a small pinch of salt, the grated lemon rind (only the yellow surface, because the white part is bitter) and finally, the hot milk little by little while continuing to stir. Cook the cream on a low flame while mixing

without stopping. When it has thickened continue cooking for about another 2 minutes.

Then take the mixture off the flame and let it cool, stirring from time to time.

CROSTATA ALLA FRUTTA
(Fruit tart)

Crostata is a tart made with shortcrust pastry generally filled with jam or a cream. The following tart is cream-filled and decorated with fresh fruit.

It can be found in pastry shops all over Italy, and many families also often make them at home.

So light and pleasant, it is gradually beginning to replace the usual wedding cake at receptions.

Fruit in syrup can also be used rather than fresh fruit although this gives a somewhat different result.

Ingredients (For 4) :

Flour   1 ¹/₂ cups (200 g)
Sugar   ¹/₂ cup (100 g)

Crostata alla frutta

Butter	*¹/₂ cup (100 g)*
Fresh fruit	*14 oz (400 g)*

One cup of pastry cream,
  one egg yolk, one lemon,
  unflavored gelatine

Preparation:

Make the pastry cream as in the preceding recipe, then prepare the dough by blending the flour, sugar and small pieces of butter with your fingertips. Work quickly to obtain a crumbly texture. Then add the grated lemon rind and the egg yolks.

Knead together quickly until you get a smooth, homogeneous dough (if necessary add a little very cold water). But you must work the dough as little as possible, otherwise the butter gets too warm and will tend to form crumbs. Wrap the dough in wax paper and let it rest in the refrigerator for half an hour. Then roll out with a rolling pin into a disk ¹/₈ inch in thickness and line a round, low cake tin with it. Prick holes in the crust with a fork (otherwise the dough will swell and form bubbles when baking).

Bake in a 350° F (180°C) oven until it turns golden. Let it cool before removing it from the tin.

Meanwhile wash and peel the fruit (tangerines, bananas, strawberries, kiwis, etc.) and slice. Sprinkle the fruit (that tends to turn black such as bananas) with lemon juice.

Fill the crust with the cold pastry cream and arrange the fruit over the cream in regular concentric circles alternating colors for decoration.

Spread a thin layer of gelatine over the fruit to make it shiny.

Let it cool and set, then serve.

If you cannot find...

Gelatine: you can omit, as it is only for decoration.

Crostata alla ricotta

CROSTATA ALLA RICOTTA
(Ricotta tart)

This excellent tart comes from Latium, but it is also common in other central Italian regions (Marches, Abruzzo) and, with some differences, in Campania too. There, with a very elaborate filling which also makes use of cooked wheat, it becomes a sumptuous dessert under the name of Pastiera napoletana *(Neapolitan Easter cake). The* ricotta *tart can be embellished by the addition of small pieces of bitter chocolate, chopped almonds, or crumbled almond macaroons.*

Ingredients *(For 4) :*
For the shortcrust pastry:

Flour	1 2/3 cups	(250 g)
Butter	1/2 cup	(125 g)
Sugar	1/2 cup	(100 g)

2 egg yolks
Grated rind of one lemon

For the filling:

Ricotta *cheese*	11 oz	(300 g)
Sugar	1/2 cup	(100 g)

Raisins	2 oz	(50 g)
Mixed candied fruits	2 oz	(50 g)
Pine nuts	1 oz	(30 g)

2 eggs

One lemon, cinnamon, salt

Preparation:

Make the short crust pastry as indicated in the preceding recipe (see "Fruit tart").

While this is setting in the refrigerator, prepare the filling. Soak the raisins in warm water for half an hour, then dry them and roll lightly in flour. Mix the *ricotta* with the sugar and the egg yolks, the grated lemon rind, and a tablespoon of lemon juice. Add the raisins, candied fruit, and pine nuts. Whip the egg whites with a pinch of salt and stir them gently into the cheese mixture folding from bottom to top. Roll out the pastry to about 1/8 inch thickness and put into a lightly buttered cake tin.

Pour the *ricotta* cream into the crust and with strips of the left-over pastry make a criss-cross on the upper crust. If you like, you can brush some beaten egg yolk onto the crust.

Bake in a 350° F (180° C) oven for about an hour. Let the tart cool before removing it from the tin.

If you cannot find...
Ricotta: use cottage cheese or anything similar.

DOLCE AGLI AMARETTI
(Almond macaroon cream)

This is a fairly new dessert which exists in various versions and has no precise regional connotations.
It is a good example of the creamy kind of dessert that has had enormous success in recent decades and is easily found in most Italian restaurants as well as on family tables.
This dessert is particularly suitable at the end of a good lunch.

Ingredients *(For 4)* :

Whipping cream	9 oz	(250 g)
Sugar	1/2 cup	(100 g)
Almond macaroons	5 oz	(150 g)

4 very fresh egg yolks

Rum or brandy

Preparation:

Make a powder of the macaroons by putting them through the blender or crushing them with a rolling pin. Beat the egg yolks vigorously with the sugar (best done with an electric beater) until they are light and foamy. Then mix in the macaroon powder and a liqueur glass of rum or brandy. Whip the cream until firm and add it to the cream, blending delicately by folding from bottom to top. Pour the cream into a mold lined with aluminum foil and place in the freezer for 2-3 hours. Take it out of the freezer 15-20 minutes before serving.

If you cannot find...
Almond macaroons: substitute with 5 ounces of finely chopped peeled almonds and half a phial of almond extract.

DOLCETTI DI MANDORLE
(Almond cookies)

Almonds are one of the common ingredients of many traditional Italian pastries, because they are produced in such great quantities in various regions (Abruzzo, Sicily, Sardinia). There are many local variations of these pastries as well. We have chosen a version that is quite similar to the famous Amaretti (Macaroons).

Ingredients (For 4) :

Powdered sugar	1 cup (200 g)
Skinned almonds	4 1/2 oz (120 g)
4 egg whites	
Almond extract, granulated	
sugar, butter, vanilla, salt	

Preparation:

Chop the almonds very finely, or better, reduce them to a powder in the blender. Mix with the sugar, a few drops of almond extract, a pinch of vanilla powder, and 2 egg whites (not whipped). Whip the other 2 egg whites to a dry, firm consistency with a pinch of salt, then blend them with the almond mixture, mixing carefully from bottom to top so that they do not break. Butter the oven pan or a cookie sheet and put little knobs of the mixture on it at a good distance one from the other. Sprinkle them with a little powdered sugar and bake in about a 320°F (160° C) oven for approximately 15 minutes. Remove the cookies and let them cool.
If stored quite dry, they will keep for several days.

FRITTELLE DI RISO
(Rice pancakes)

Making sweet pastries from rice is a Tuscan specialty. Besides small tarts of shortcrust pastry filled with rice cooked in milk and flavored with orange, there are also these delicious pancakes which have the advantage of being quite easy to make.

Ingredients (For 4) :

Milk	1 pint (1/2 liter)
Rice	4 oz (100 g)
Flour	1/3 cup (50 g)
Sugar	1/2 cup (100 g)
Raisins	2 oz (50 g)
Candied orange peel	1 oz (25 g)
Butter	2 tablespoons
One egg, one lemon, salt, a sweet	
liqueur, oil for frying	

Preparation:

Bring the milk to a boil together with a tablespoon of sugar, pinch of salt, the grated rind of one lemon (only the yellow part because the white is very bitter), and the butter. Then add the rice and cook until the milk has been entirely absorbed. Let it cool. Meanwhile soak the raisins in warm water for half an hour. Add the egg yolk to the rice and a tablespoon of liqueur, the raisins which have been dried after soaking, small pieces of the orange peel, and the flour. Whip the egg white to a dry, firm consistency and fold in delicately. Heat a good amount of oil in a frying pan and drop in spoonfuls of the batter, letting them turn golden on both sides. Put them on paper for a moment to absorb the oil and serve hot, sprinkled with the remaining sugar.

PANNA COTTA
(Cream custard)

This smooth creamy dessert from Piedmont has only recently been rediscovered and is having huge success all over Italy. There is no restaurant which does not have it on its dessert menu. There are also various commercial versions available, and it is very fast and easy to make at home. Panna cotta can be served with caramel, fruit (strawberry, kiwi, etc.), or chocolate sauce.

Ingredients *(For 4)* :
Fresh whipping cream	*1 pt (1/2 liter)*
Milk	*1/2 pt (1/4 liter)*
Sugar	*3/4 cup (175 g)*
Gelatine	*1/2 oz (12 g)*
Vanilla	

Preparation:
Soften a strip of gelatine in cold water for 10 minutes then squeeze out the water and put in a pot with the cream, milk, a packet of powdered vanilla and 3 tablespoons of sugar. Heat the mixture, stirring until the gelatine and the sugar are perfectly dissolved. Pour the mixture into a rectangular mold moistened with water (or else individual custard molds) and refrigerate for 3-4 hours. Shortly before serving, caramelize the remaining sugar in very little water. Stir continuously and take off the flame when the sugar has dissolved and turned golden.
Reverse the molded custard onto a serving plate (or individual little plates) and pour a little caramel sauce onto each portion.

PERE AL VINO CON ZABAIONE
(Pears cooked in wine with zabaione)

Zabaione is an exquisite cream of Piedmontese origin that is also used in pastries as a filling for cream puffs, doughnuts, etc. It is delicious eaten hot or cold together with light cookies or cooked fruit. In the recipe that follows, it is used in a typically Piedmontese way with pears cooked in a robust red wine of the kind for which Piedmont is justly famous.

Ingredients *(For 4)* :
Sugar	*1 cup (200 g)*
2 ripe pears	
4 egg yolks	
Robust red wine	*1 pt (1/2 liter)*
Marsala wine, half a lemon, cinnamon	

Preparation:
In a deep but not wide pot, where the pears can stand upright and very near each other, boil the red wine for 15 minutes together with about half a glass of water, a stick of cinnamon, a few pieces of lemon peel (only the yellow part) and half the sugar.
Peel but do not cut the pears, immerse them in the wine syrup and cook slowly for 20-30 minutes until they are soft but still fairly firm.
Let them cool in their liqueur.
Meanwhile prepare the *zabaione*.
Beat the egg yolks vigorously with the remaining sugar, then add little by little 8 tablespoons of Marsala wine and cook the cream in a double-boiler without ever letting the water boil, stirring continuously.
After about 15 minutes when the *zabaione* has greatly increased, remove from the fire and serve it on the drained pears.

If you cannot find...
Marsala: use the wine in which the pears have been cooked, or Madeira or sherry.

Pesche ripiene
(Fillled peaches)

Given the abundance of fruit all Italian regions can count on in all seasons, and particularly in summer, it is no surprise if during the course of centuries, many recipes have been invented for desserts made with fruit. Among the many recipes for filled peaches, the following one is the most common. It is easy to make and very pleasant, especially at the end of a summer lunch. A winter version can be made by substituting apples for the pears.

Ingredients *(For 4)* :
4 large ripe peaches
Sugar   ⅛ cup   (30 g)
Almond macaroons   4 oz (100 g)
One egg yolk, butter, unsweetened
  cocoa

Preparation:
Wash the fruit well and cut in half without peeling. Remove the pits and spoon out the cavity a little to enlarge it. Put the extracted pulp in a blender and mix it with the egg yolk, the finely crushed macaroons, a teaspoon of cocoa and one of sugar. Fill the peach halves with some of the mixture, place in an oven dish and bake at 350° F (180° C) for about half an hour. Serve cold, possibly together with vanilla ice cream if you like.

Salame dolce
(Sweet "salami")

Originating in Emilia, this sweet is a favorite, especially among children, and is very easy to make. Its name is dictated not only by its shape but also by the pieces of biscuit it contains which imitate the pieces of lard in real salame.

Ingredients *(For 4)* :
Unsweetened cocoa   2 oz   (50 g)
Dry cookies   7 oz (200 g)
Butter   ½ cup (150 g)
Sugar   ¼ cup   (70 g)
2 very fresh egg yolks
Sweet anise liqueur

Preparation:
Crush the cookies into not overly small irregular pieces. Mix them with the melted butter, the sugar, cocoa, the egg yolks and a liqueur glass of the anise. Blend well and put the mixture on a piece of aluminum foil, shape into a salami sausage, and roll tightly in the foil. Let it harden well in the refrigerator for 2-3 hours and serve sliced.

Tirami su

This creamy, coffee-flavored and high-calorie dessert (its name "give me a boost" is, in this sense, very meaningful) is rapidly becoming Italy's national dessert.
A quite recent invention (apparently originating in Veneto), it immediately had enormous success, and now there is no restaurant that does not have it

on its list of desserts. It is also made industrially, but these are quite far from the original recipe. Its fame is spreading outside Italy due to the many tourists who tried it and fell in love with it. Tirami su *is very easy to make if you can manage to find its basic ingredient which is* mascarpone. *If not ,you can substitute with any other sweet, creamy cheese, even though the result will be a little different.*

Ingredients *(For 4)* :

Mascarpone	*14 oz (400 g)*
Sponge cake	*14 oz (400 g)*
Sugar	*1 cup (200 g)*

2 very fresh eggs
2 egg yolks
Unsweetened cocoa, strong coffee

Tirami su

Preparation:

Beat the egg yolks with the sugar until light and fluffy, then blend well with the *mascarpone.*
Whip the egg whites to a firm consistency and add to the cream, mixing carefully from bottom to top so they do not break.

Cut the sponge cake into thin slices and soak with the coffee. In glass cups or in a rectangular pyrex dish, alternate layers of sponge cake with cream, ending up with the latter. Powder with cocoa passed through a sieve and put in the refrigerator for a few hours before serving.

If you cannot find...
Mascarpone: you can use any other fresh cheese such as cottage cheese or cream cheese.

Torrone
(Italian nougat)

Although torrone *is a candy that is usually produced on an industrial scale, or at least a commercial one, it can also be made with good results at home. It requires a bit of skill, time and patience, but it can be a source of great satisfaction to produce this candy at home, which in Italy is a symbol of Christmas.*

Ingredients *(For 4) :*

Peeled almonds	11 oz	(300 g)
Peeled hazel nuts	5 oz	(150 g)
Light-colored honey	7 oz	(200 g)
Sugar	1 cup	(200 g)
2 egg whites		
Wafers		
Vanilla		

Preparation:
Cook the honey with a pinch of powdered vanilla in a rather large double-boiler on a low flame and stir with a wooden spoon. The honey must be cooked until it breaks like ice when some is dropped into cold water. At that point whip the egg whites and add the honey to it little by little. Then put it back on the flame and cook to the same point again (where it breaks like ice in cold water). Caramelize the sugar in another pot with very little water. As soon as it turns liquid and golden in color, pour it little by little into the honey mixture, blending well. Add the almonds and hazel nuts and mix them until they are evenly distributed in the sweet mixture. Spread on a sheet of wafer, giving it a regular form (rectangular and about $1/3$ inch high), with the help of two broad-bladed knives, then cover with another sheet of wafer and press lightly. Cut into pieces, they will keep for many days in a tin box.

Torta di Carote
(Carrot cake)

This cake, originating in the Tridentine-South Tyrol, is very simple and healthy. It is particularly recommended as an afternoon snack or at breakfast because of its high energy content.

Ingredients *(For 4) :*

Four	1 3/4 cups	(250 g)
Granulated sugar	2 1/4 cups	(250 g)
Butter	1/2 cup	(150 g)
Grated carrots	9 oz	(250 g)
Peeled almonds	5 oz	(150 g)
4 eggs		
Baking powder	2 teaspoons	
Powdered sugar, one lemon		

Preparation:
Beat the eggs with the sugar then add the flour, the melted butter, the grated rind of the lemon, the carrots, the finely chopped almonds and the baking powder.
Pour the dough into a buttered, floured cake mould and bake in a 350° F (180° C) oven for 35-40 minutes. When the cake has cooled, sprinkle it with powdered sugar and serve.

Torta di Mele Casalinga
(Homemade apple cake)

Apple cake is perhaps the most common dessert there is, and not only in Italy.

There are infinite recipes for it, since practically every family has its own favorite, that may have been handed down through the generations.
In Italy a rather soft, spongy kind of apple cake is the favorite.
The following recipe is a typical example.

Ingredients (For 4) :

Apples	1 $^3/4$ lb (750 g)
Flour	1 heaping cup (150g)
Sugar	$^3/4$ cup (150 g)
Butter	8 tablespoons
2 eggs	
Baking powder	1 teaspoon
Marsala, one lemon	

Preparation:

Peel and slice the apples and mix in 2 tablespoons of sugar and a liqueur glass of marsala.

Beat the eggs with the remaining sugar, add the flour, the melted butter, the grated lemon rind and finally the apples drained of their juice.

Pour into a buttered cake mould and bake in a 350° F (180° C) oven for 35-40 minutes.

Torta di mele casalinga

TORTA DI RISO
(Rice cake)

This nutritious dessert is a traditional Emilian recipe, in particular Bologna where it is still called Torta degli addobbi *("Decorations cake") because it was traditionally prepared on holidays when it was customary to hang colored banners from windows and balconies.*

Ingredients *(For 4) :*

Rice	*7 oz (200 g)*
Milk	*1/2 pt (1/4 liter)*
Sugar	*3/4 cup (150 g)*
Butter	*3 1/2 tablespoons*

2 eggs
One orange, one lemon, salt,
  breadcrumbs, anise liqueur

Preparation:
Boil the rice in slightly salted water for 5 minutes, then drain and let it cool.
Bring the milk with an equal amount of water to a boil together with the sugar and the butter. Add the rice and cook until all the liquid has been

Torta millefoglie

absorbed. Let it cool to tepid, then add the egg yolks, the grated rind of one lemon and half an orange, and, at the end, the egg whites whipped to a peak. Pour this mixture into a buttered cake mold which has been sprinkled with the breadcrumbs, then cook in a 350° F (180° C) oven for about half an hour. Let the cake cool before removing from the mold and serving.

Torta MILLEFOGLIE
(Puff-pastry cream cake)

Ingredients:

Frozen puff pastry	*1 lb*	*(500 g)*
Whipping cream	*9 oz*	*(250 g)*
Milk	*1 pt*	*(¹/₂ liter)*
Granulated sugar	*¹/₂ cup*	*(100 g)*
Flour	*¹/₃ cup*	*(50 g)*
Peeled almonds	*2 oz*	*(50 g)*

4 egg yolks
Powdered sugar, lemon

Preparation:

Let the puff pastry thaw at room temperature, then roll it out into 3 very thin disks or rectangles. Pierce with a fork and bake on a sheet in a 370° F (190° C) oven for about 20 minutes until slightly golden in color. Beat the egg yolks with the sugar, add the flour, a bit of grated lemon rind, and dilute gradually with hot milk. Cook this custard for a few minutes on a low flame until it has become completely thickened. Let it cool. Whip the cream to a firm consistency, add the powdered sugar and blend this carefully with the custard. On a serving dish place the puff pastry disks or rectangles one on top of the other spreading the cream between the layers. Also spread cream around the sides. Cut the almonds into very thin slices, toast them for a few minutes in the oven and apply to the sides of the cake. Serve the dessert cold with a little powdered sugar sprinkled over the top.

Torta PARADISO
(Paradise cake)

This cake is so named because it is exceptionally light and soft. It originates in Lombardy and can be served with tea or sweet wine according to the occasion. It is often filled with a cream.

Ingredients *(For 4)* :

Corn starch	*4 oz*	*(100 g)*
Flour	*¹/₂ cup*	*(75 g)*
Granulated sugar	*8 oz*	*(200 g)*

5 eggs
Powdered sugar, butter,
  baking powder, lemon, salt

Preparation:

Beat the egg yolks with the granulated sugar until they are fluffy and foamy. Add the flour, the corn starch, the grated lemon rind and a teaspoon of baking powder. Whip the egg whites to a firm consistency with a pinch of salt and carefully blend them with the dough, folding from bottom to top. Pour the dough into a buttered and floured cake mold and bake in a 320° F (160° C) oven for about an hour. Let it cool, then sprinkle with powdered sugar.

Zuccotto

This dessert gets its name from its shape reminiscent of a clerical skull-cap.
It originally comes from Florence, but is now native to all of Italy, particularly in its version as an ice-cream cake.

Ingredients *(For 4) :*

Whipping cream	*12 oz*	*(350 g)*
Sponge cake	*12 oz*	*(350 g)*
Powdered sugar	*3 oz*	*(75 g)*
Bitter chocolate	*1½ oz*	*(40 g)*
Mixed candied fruits	*1 ½ oz*	
Sugar	*3 oz*	
Unsweetened cocoa	*1½ oz*	
2 eggs		
Any sweet liqueur		

Preparation:

Cut the top crust off the sponge cake and cut the rest in thin slices, then moisten them with a little liqueur diluted in water.
Whip the cream to a thick consistency and sweeten with the sugar.
Divide the cream into two unequal parts.
Add the sifted cocoa and the chocolate cut into bits to the white cream.

With about ²/₃ of the sponge cake slices, line the inside of a half-sphere mould. Pour the white cream into it leaving a cavity in the center into which you will put the chocolate cream.

Cover this with the remaining sponge cake and keep the cake in the refrigerator for 6-8 hours (or in the freezer for 2-3 hours) before serving.

Zuccotto

Zuppa inglese
("English soup")

Originating in Tuscany and Emilia Romagna, this dessert is by now widely found and much liked everywhere. In Italy the liqueur most used to make zuppa inglese *is Alchermes, with its characteristic red color. But you may also use any other liqueur.*

Ingredients *(For 4) :*

Sponge cake	14 oz	(400 g)
Milk	1 qt	(1 liter)
Flour	4 oz	(100 g)
Sugar	9 oz	(250 g)
Bitter cocoa	2 oz	(40 g)

2 eggs
Grated lemon rind or vanilla, coffee, any liqueur

Zuppa inglese

Preparation:

Beat the eggs with the sugar until they are fluffy and foamy, then add the flour. Dilute this slowly with the hot milk, adding it a little at a time. Flavor with the grated lemon rind or vanilla and cook this cream on a medium flame stirring it without stopping until it has become thick and lost the taste of raw flour.

Divide it in two parts. Add the cocoa to one half of the cream and mix it well. Cut the sponge cake into rather thin slices and pour sweetened coffee on some of them. Put these into a large glass dish and pour on half the dark cream.

Make another layer of sliced cake moistened with liqueur and pour on half the yellow cream.

Continue making layers in this way until you have used up the ingredients. Keep the dessert in the refrigerator for a few hours before serving.

A typical Italian restaurant: Otello alla Concordia *on Via della Croce, Rome.*

REGIONAL DISHES

A list of all the regional Italian specialties in their infinite variety would require much more space than we have available. In the recipe section of this book we have necessarily limited ourselves to a fairly complete panorama of the most typical dishes, the ones that best give an idea of Italian cuisine. In addition, we have also thought it useful to present a brief introduction describing the characteristics of each province's cuisine and a very brief description of its other typical dishes. For each dish we indicate what course it is and its principal ingredients.

ABRUZZO AND MOLISE

Rustic, tasty, and somewhat sharp cooking due to the quite wide use of hot red chili pepper, this cuisine offers no particular specialties, but is marked by its genuine and distinct flavors.
It is divided into two parts, the coastal area where fish is of course prominent, and the mountains where pork, cured meats and cheese predominate.
Pastries are noteworthy which exploit the abundant almond production of the area.

Cassata all'abruzzese: Dessert. A soft layer-cake soaked in the local liqueur (*centerbe*) that alternates layers of

---

CONVERSION TABLE

Weight measurements
(Values rounded off to the nearest 25 grams)

Ounces	Grams	Ounces	Grams
1	25	9	250
2	50	10	275
3	75	11	300
4	100	12	350
5	150	13	375
6	175	14	400
7	200	15	425
8	225	16 (1 lb)	450

American measurements used in *Al Dente* have the following equivalences:

American liquid measurements
16 fl oz = 0.47 liters   1 qt = 0.94 liters
 1 pt   = 0.47 liters   1 gal = 3.78 liters

American dry measurements
Flour $3/4$ cups =   100 g
Sugar $1/2$ cups =   100 g
Butter $1/2$ cups
  or 8 tablespoons = 100 g

butter cream and chocolate chips with *torrone* (see the section "Typical Products").

Maccheroni alla chitarra: First course. A kind of egg pasta spaghetti generally served in a sauce of tomato, bacon and onion, or else a lamb stew. Very tasty.

Parrozzo: Dessert. A pastry without liqueur or cream, soft and aromatic and covered with chocolate.

Scamorza ai ferri: Main course. A typical local cheese is cut into thick slices and grilled, then served hot and slightly melted.

Scrippelle: First course. An omelette cut into strips and served in a meat broth.

APULIA

The cooking of this region is distinctly Mediterranean in being almost exclusively composed of vegetables, fish and seafood, oil, cheeses, and pasta. Meat takes a definite back seat except for lamb. The crusty, country bread is excellent.

Carteddate: Dessert. These are thin strips of fried dough covered with honey.

Copete: Dessert. Cookies of almond and sugar.

Lampascioni al forno: A baked appetizer and side dish. This is a kind of bitter onion that grows in the region.

Melanzane alla campagnola (Country-style eggplant): Appetizer or side dish. Slices of eggplant broiled and seasoned with garlic and aromatic herbs. Very fragrant and tasty.

Minestra di fave (Broad bean soup): First course. A very simple and delicate dish which can be slightly bitter if the vegetables include chicory leaves.

Orata alla barese (Bari-style gilthead): Main course. In this exquisite recipe the fish is cooked in the oven with potatoes, herbs and *pecorino* cheese.

Orecchiette alle cime di rapa (Orecchiette with turnip greens): First course. Usually a homemade pasta eaten with this vegetable very popular in Apulia, it is seasoned with garlic and hot red peppers browned in oil. Slightly sharp.

Tiella di riso (Rice platter): First course. A rich dish of rice, mussels, potatoes and sometimes tomatoes.

Tortiera di alici (Baked anchovies): Appetizer or main course. Fresh anchovies baked in the oven with breadcrumbs, herbs, and of course, oil.

CALABRIA AND BASILICATA

In this region, as in others, the food is divided into two categories, "land food" and "sea food." Meat is limited almost entirely to pork and lamb.

Prominent among the vegetables are eggplant, bell peppers, and tomatoes.

The coastal areas naturally make the most of fish and seafood.

There is also an ample choice of cured meats and cheeses.

Calabria and Basilicata are the regions that make the greatest use of red hot chili peppers

Baccalà alla lucana (Stockfish Lucana-style): Main course. The fish is cooked in a pan with marinated bell peppers. Rather strong tasting.

Bracioline di pesce spada (Swordfish steaks): The slices of fish are wrapped around a filling of mozzarella, breadcrumbs and herbs, then cooked in wine.

Macco di fave: First course. A broad bean soup with onion and tomatoes.

Sarde a scapece: Appetizer or main course. The sardines are fried, garnished in breadcrumbs and a very hot mixture of oil, vinegar and herbs, then left to cool. A strong-flavored and aromatic dish.

Zuppa di pesce di Maratea (Fish soup): Unlike similar recipes from other regions, this fish soup is generally made without tomato or garlic. Instead onion and parsley are used.

CAMPANIA

The cuisine of Campania is among the most famous abroad and can boast being the birthplace of the best known Italian dishes such as spaghetti with tomato sauce and pizza.

It has a wealth of other dishes, however, among which first place goes to vegetable ones such as eggplant, tomatoes, and bell peppers and to fish and seafood dishes.

Mozzarella also holds a prominent place, especially the kind made from water buffalo's milk.

Meat is used in relatively few recipes, but one cannot forget to include *ragout*, a thick tomato sauce in which beef or pork is simmered after which the meat is removed and served separately.

Cecenielli fritti: Appetizer. Tiny fish which are fried in a batter.

Melanzane ripiene (Stuffed eggplant): Appetizer. There are many versions of this dish, but one of the most common is when the vegetable is split in half and filled with mozzarella, breadcrumbs and tomato. It is then generally baked in the oven.

Pastiera: A rich pastry dough filled with a soft *ricotta* cream, wheat, and eggs, with a delicate orange fragrance.

EMILIA-ROMAGNA

The cuisine of this region is among the richest in Italy with its large and varied production of cured meats and excellent cheeses. The Parma-Reggio Emilia area is dominated by many egg pasta dishes and is also rich in hearty meat courses. On the Romagna coast there is fine fish, and everywhere wonderful bread, which should not be forgotten. The most famous Emilian dishes, known and appreciated everywhere, have long been part of the whole country's gastronomic heritage.

Bomba di riso: First course. A rich rice mould filled with pigeon meat.

Calzagatti: First course. This is a soft polenta served with a tasty bean, bacon and tomato sauce.

Cotechino in camicia: Main course. *Cotechino*, a traditional cooked sausage, becomes the filling of a savory roast that is often cooked in Lambrusco, the red Emilian wine.

Gnocco fritto (Fried gnocchi): Appetizer. Thin and crispy pasta squares served with a local *salame* and sparkling Lambrusco wine.

Passatelli: First course. Soft little dumplings made of breadcrumbs and cheese, served in a meat broth.

Scaloppine alla Bolognese (Escalopes Bolognese): Main course. Turkey or veal slices cooked in butter, then covered with cured *prosciutto* or *mortadella* and fresh parmesan cheese and put briefly in the oven.

FRIULI-VENEZIA GIULIA

This is for the most part quite simple cuisine, making wide use of pork and beans as well as polenta.
Excellent wines and cured meats (among them the delicious *San Daniele prosciutto*) and cheeses are produced in this region.

Cialzons: First course. A kind of egg pasta stuffed with a sweet-sour filling generally of potatoes.
Melted butter and local cheese are the usual condiments.

Frico: Main course. Local cheese sliced and fried alone or with onions.

Gubana: Dessert. Puff pastry filled with dried fruit.

Musetto e bravade: Main course. A hearty dish of a kind

of cooked *salame* with cooked turnips. Very tasty.

Presnitz: Dessert. A rich pastry filled with dried fruit.

LATIUM

The gastronomic tradition of Latium is very popular and particularly emphasizes simple, rustic pasta dishes, main courses of lamb or offal, artichokes, and the omnipresent aroma of garlic. But there is no lack of fish and seafood either.
Noteworthy among the latter are jumbo shrimp locally called *mazzancolle* which are generally grilled.
In Rome, by now the general trend is towards a generic kind of cuisine that has lost its local characteristics, but it is not hard to find places that still offer traditional Roman dishes.

Abbacchio a scottadito (Lamb chops): Main course. Tender young lamb chops cooked on a brazier.

Abbacchio brodettato (Lamb stew): Stewed lamb served in a sauce of egg, lemon juice, and herbs. Particularly delicate.

Carciofi alla romana (Artichokes Roman-style): Side dish. Large artichokes cooked and flavored with garlic and mint.

Coda alla vaccinara (Ox tail stew): Main course. A very tasty oxtail dish stewed in a sauce of tomato, celery and other vegetables.

Pollo alla romana (Roman-style chicken): Main course. Pieces of chicken cooked in a delicious bell pepper sauce.

Pomodori al riso (Tomatoes with rice): First course. Large tomatoes stuffed with rice and baked in the oven.

Puntarelle all'acciuga: Side dish. A crunchy, tasty salad green dressed in an anchovy-garlic sauce.

Rigatoni con la pajata: First course. Pasta in a tasty sauce of suckling lamb's intestines.

Spaghetti alla gricia: First course. Pasta in a sauce of oil, bacon and onion, plus grated cheese and pepper.

Spaghetti cacio e pepe (Cheese and peppers spaghetti): First course. Simple and delicious dish of pasta served only with oil, *pecorino* and black pepper. Slightly sharp in flavor.

LIGURIA

Ligurian cuisine is primarily based on fish, aromatic herbs and vegetables, as well as the region's excellent olive oil.

Many dishes, from *minestrone* to *lasagna*, are often flavored by adding Genoese *pesto* (see the recipe for *Trenette al pesto* in the section on "Dried Pasta"). Rabbit is the most popular meat. Ligurian cooking is the lightest in all Italy.

Cappon magro: Appetizer or main course. A rich salad composed of many kinds of fish, seafood, vegetables, and mushrooms dressed with a very tasty sauce.

Cima alla genovese: Main course. One of the rare typical dishes made with beef, this is a "pocket" filled with offal that is then boiled and served in slices.

Farinata: Appetizer. A kind of pizza made with chick-pea flour.

Pansotti al pesto di noci: First course. Egg pasta stuffed with vegetables and *ricotta*, dressed in a sauce of nuts, cream, oil, and cheese. Very delicate.

Torta pasqualina (Easter pie): Appetizer. A very delicate savory pie made of spinach, *ricotta*, and eggs. There are also less usual kinds, but equally delicious, with a filling of artichokes, for example.

LOMBARDY

The food of this region differs considerably from one province to another.
One common characteristic is the prevalence of meat and vegetables, however, Lombardy lakes also provide freshwater fish for quite a few dishes.
The principle condiment in the rice dishes is butter.
The ample cheese production is obviously reflected in the region's recipes too.

Busecca: First course. A hearty dish made of tripe and beans that is rustic and tasty.

Cassoeula: Main course. A typical country-style winter dish of stewed pork, sausage, and cabbage. Not recommended for those with delicate stomachs!

Pizzoccheri alla valtellinese: First course. A *tagliatelle* kind of pasta (see the section "Pasta") made of dark flour and a sauce of butter, cheese, and vegetables.

Polenta e osei: One-course meal. The polenta is eaten with roast fowl and their cooking juice.

Riso alla pilota: First course. A specialty of Mantua where the rice is eaten in a sausage sauce.

Risotto alla certosina: First course. A rich dish of rice with frog meat, shrimps, mushrooms and peas. Very delicate.

Stufato/Stracotto: A beef stew cooked with vegetables in wine or broth and simmered until very tender. It is served in its sauce.

Torta sbrisolona: Dessert. This lumpy-looking cake is crunchy and crumbly. It is usually served with cream or *zabaione* (see the section "Sweets and Pastries").

Tortelli di zucca: First course. Egg pasta filled with a sweet mixture of yellow squash and tomato puree. Dressed with butter and grated cheese.

MARCHES

The coastal regions, of course, offer many fish dishes, while inland you find a hearty cuisine generously seasoned.

Brodetto: Fish soup with an onion flavor. There are, however, many variations of this dish.

Ravioli all'anconetana (Ravioli Ancona-style): First course. Stuffed egg pasta that owes its particular flavor to the filling of cheese, lemon rind, and a pinch of sugar. It is cooked and then put under the broiler.

Stoccafisso in potacchio: Main course. Stockfish cooked in a thick tomato sauce and then put in the oven with potatoes.

Vincisgrassi: First course. A rich dish similar to *lasagne* (see the section "Pasta") in which layers of egg pasta alternate with an abundant sauce of veal offal, tomato and bechamel sauce.

PIEDMONT AND VALLE D'AOSTA

These regions produce excellent wines and cheeses which, of course, play the leading roles in several great recipes. Another important ingredient is rice, a great quantity of which is produced in Piedmont.
The most refined dishes rarely do without white truffles. Meat dishes prevail although there are also some preparations for freshwater fish from the region's lakes. During the season one should note the abundance of mushrooms that are found in the Alpine woods.

Antipasti misti (Vegetable appetizers): Bell peppers and other vegetables conserved in oil, often homemade.

Bonet: Dessert. A soft chocolate pudding.

Carne all'albese: An appetizer or main course. Very lean ground raw beef which is marinated in lemon juice and dressed with oil, salt, pepper and grated truffle.

Paniscia/Panissa: First course. A hearty dish made of rice, beans and pork.

Polenta concia: A one-dish meal. Polenta (see the recipe section "Appetizers") is dressed with butter and cheeses, among which figures *fontina* from the Val d'Aosta, of course.

Rostone: Main course. A very delicate roast beef served in a cream sauce and, usually, with truffles.

Torta Gianduia: Dessert. A sumptuous chocolate nutcake.

SARDINIA

Bread is one of the most distinctive elements of Sardinian food and it is found in special, characteristic forms such as *carta da musica* (music paper) or *pane carasau*.

Other basic products come from sheep raising, such as lamb meat and cheeses, as well as fish and pasta.

Burrida: Appetizer. A rich mixed fish salad dressed in a sauce of oil, vinegar and herbs.

Cordula: Main course. A tasty dish of lamb offal sometimes served with peas.

Gallina al mirto (Hen in myrtle): Main course. A hen is boiled and then covered with myrtle leaves for 1-2 days so it becomes very aromatic.

Maccarones con bottarga (Macaroni with mullet roe): First course. Homemade pasta served with mullet roe, *bottarga* (see "Typical Products").

Maiale alla brace (Roast pig): Main course. A pig is roasted on a spit over a strongly aromatic brazier. The same roasting is used for lamb.

Malloreddus: First course. Small pasta seasoned with saffron, tomato sauce and *ricotta*.

Pane frattau: Starter. This delicate and crunchy local bread is flavored with tomato, egg, oil and cheese.

Pardulas: Dessert. Delicate pastries filled with a fresh cheese cream, flavored with lemon and saffron.

Trattaliu: Main course. Lamb's intestines cooked on a spit or in the oven and flavored with dill.

SICILY

The cuisine of this region is of a richly composite kind with evident North African influences.

It naturally puts much more emphasis on fish, vegetables and pasta than on meat.

Sicilian cooking often tends to sweet-and-sour flavors by adding raisins, and in general the sauces are less sharp than in other parts of the South.

Cuscus: First course. A clearly North African dish made of a very small, granular kind of pasta and usually served with a fish soup or lamb stew and a lot of vegetables.

Farsumagru: Beef rolls stuffed with *salami*, egg, cheese, and simmered in a tomato sauce.

Gelo di melone (Jellied melon): Dessert. This is a kind of watermelon gelatine with bits of candied fruit and chocolate. The same kind of dessert is sometimes made with other flavors such as coffee, lemon, etc.

Maccaruni di casa: First course. A homemade flour-and-water pasta generally served in a meat and tomato sauce. Very flavorful.

Pasta con le sarde (Pasta with sardines): First course. A sweet-and-sour pasta made with fresh fish, raisins and aromatic herbs.

Pasta 'ncasciata: First course. Pasta in a sauce of meat, hard-boiled egg and cheese, then put in the oven.

Pesce al salmoriglio: Main course. The fish is roasted then dressed in a tasty sauce of oil, lemon, parsley, garlic and oregano.

Sarde a beccafico: Appetizer or main course. Sardines are stuffed with breadcrumbs and herbs then baked in the oven or fried.

Vermicelli alla siracusana (Vermicelli Syracuse-style): First course. A spaghetti-type pasta in a sauce of tomato, bell peppers, eggplant, olives, and capers.

TRIDENTINE-SOUTH TYROL

The cuisine of these two regions is similar: mountain cooking using a lot of pork, sausages, cheeses, and polenta. For some years dry pasta (*maccheroni*, spaghetti, etc.) has been in use in all homes and most restaurants, but it is foreign to the traditions of the region. An Austrian influence is quite evident, particularly in the cooking of the South Tyrol.

Canederli: First course. Large bread dumplings flavored

with aromatic herbs and speck (see the section "Typical Products") served in a meat broth or "dry" with melted butter.

Orzetto: First course. A barley soup with potatoes and other vegetables, flavored with bacon.

Smacafam: One-dish meal. Dark polenta dressed with lard and sausages. For people with excellent digestion.

Strangolapreti: Bread and spinach dumplings usually served with melted sage-flavored butter. Delicate in flavor.

Stinco di maiale (Pork shin): This cut of pork is found almost exclusively in this region. It makes a flavorful roast that is worth trying if you ever happen to be in the Tridentine.

Strudel di mele (Apple strudel): Dessert. This pastry comes from Austria, but it is also one of the most typical of this region, thanks to the local apple crop.

Trota salmonata (Salmon trout): Main course. This very delicate freshwater fish with its rosy flesh is grilled or fried in butter.

Zelten: Dessert. A rich Christmas cake made of dried fruit.

TUSCANY

Among the most varied cuisines to be found in Italy, Tuscan tradition includes the flavorful fish stews of the coastal areas to the superb beef produced in the Maremma, and the delicious vegetable soups found throughout the region. It is in any case a simple and sober style of cooking in which every dish is embellished by the excellent Tuscan olive oils and accompanied by the fine local wines, reds being the best.

Acquacotta: First course. A simple and tasty soup of sweet peppers and other vegetables, eggs, and toasted bread. When in season, boletus mushrooms are used.

Cacciucco: First course. Very flavorful tomato fish soup from Livorno.

Castagnaccio: Dessert. A flat compact cake made of chestnut flour sprinkled with raisins and pine nuts. Not too sweet.

Fagioli al fiasco (Beans in a jar): Vegetable side dish. White beans dressed with oil, garlic and sage, cooked in a special way: inside a glass jar.

Panzanella: Appetizer. A fresh and simple salad using moistened, crumbled bread, tomatoes, raw onion, herbs, and vinegar.

Pappa al pomodoro (Mashed tomatoes): First course. A soup made of tomato puree which is eaten hot or cold with a drop of oil.

Pappardelle con la lepre (*Pappardelle* with hare): First course. Wide strips of egg pasta in an aromatic and savory hare sauce.
Also very common is this pasta in a rabbit sauce.

Pici: First course. A rather soft kind of spaghetti generally eaten in a mushroom sauce.

Ribollita: First course. A simple, rustic soup of beans and cabbage with some olive oil as seasoning.

Zuppa di farro (Spelt soup): First course. Among the many vegetable soups of the region, this is one of the best. It uses a rather uncommon kind of grain, spelt, and beans, all flavored with good Tuscan olive oil, dense and tasty.

UMBRIA

A simple cuisine whose points of reference are the fine local oil, cheeses, the black truffle of Norcia, and cured meats.
Among the main courses those based on wild fowl have a prominent place.

Ciaramicola: Dessert. An Easter cake made of yeast dough and sprinkled with colored candy.

Pizza al formaggio (Cheese pizza): Appetizer. A country-style savory pizza made with cheese, eggs and *prosciutto*.

Spaghetti/Fettuccine al tartufo (Spaghetti/Fettuccine with truffle): First course. The pasta is simply seasoned with slices of truffle lightly browned in oil.

Porchetta alla perugina (Perugia roast suckling pig): Main course. Suckling pig roasted whole on a spit and seasoned with garlic and herbs.

VENETO

This region has a sea coast, an Alpine area, and a plain. Naturally its cuisine reflects these geographical differences. A common element is a great use of polenta, which however, is not nearly so common as it once was in the past. In the sea and lagoon areas, fish and seafood are of course popular. Much prized are the *granseole* (crabs), the *cape sante* (scallops), and the *peoci* (mussels).
Many kinds of farmyard fowl are raised in the plains region

(chickens, turkeys, etc.) which are found in several of the most typical recipes.

Some of the best Italian vegetables are also grown there, such as Bassano asparagus and *radicchio*, the red lettuce of Treviso.

Baccalà mantecato (Stockfish): Main course. A very delicate dish in which the fish is cooked and minced with oil and aromatic herbs until it is reduced to a kind of cream generally served on fried polenta.

Bigoli in salsa: First course. *Bigoli* are a kind of spaghetti and are eaten with an anchovy-onion sauce that is very tasty.

Bollito con salsa pearà: Second course. Boiled beef dressed in a very savory sauce of breadcrumbs, cheese, broth and quite a lot of pepper.

Pinza: Dessert. This is a cake made of cornmeal flour with raisins and pine nuts.

Risi e bisi: A dense soup of rice and peas which is savory but delicate.

Tacchino alla melagrana (Turkey with pomegranates): Main course. The fowl is roasted with its own liver and pomegranate seeds.

ALPHABETICAL INDEX OF RECIPES

Cover photograph :
A dish of the specialty *gnocchi
con le vongole veraci (gnocchi*
with small clams*).*

Translated from the Italian by :
Charles Nopar

Edited by : Sandra E. Tokunaga

Jacket design by :
Fabrizio Patucchi

Phototypeset and Photolithography:
Gescom - Viterbo (Italy)

Printed and bound by :
Tipolitografia Petruzzi Corrado & C.
Città di Castello (PG), Italy